# THE WINNING GAME PLAN

*A Proven Leadership Playbook*

*for Continuous Business Success*

Jamey Rootes

All Rights Reserved. Published 2020.
Jamey Rootes
NRG Stadium
2 NRG Park
Houston, TX 77054-1573
www.JameyRootes.com

In association with:
Elite Online Publishing
63 East 11400 South
Suite #230
Sandy, UT 84070
EliteOnlinePublishing.com
Library of Congress Control Number: 2020921611

Printed in the United States of America

ISBN: 978-1513660615 (Amazon paperback)
ISBN: 978-1513660592 (paperback)
ISBN: 978-1513660585 (hardback)
ISBN: 978-1513660608 (eBook)

*To my hero, Bob McNair.*
*I will never forget the tremendous blessing*
*he was, and continues to be,*
*to me and my family.*

## <u>In Praise for Jamey Rootes and The Winning Game Plan</u>

Jamey Rootes sits at the intersection of two of my passions—the NFL and my hometown of Houston, Texas. For the past two decades, Jamey has worked side by side with team founder Bob McNair and the McNair family to create an organization that has consistently been among the most respected and most valuable in all pro sports. This consistency of business performance is remarkable because of the natural ups and downs that occur on the football field. Cleary, something special is going on and in Jamey's book, *The Winning Game Plan*, he reveals principles that are the foundation of the Houston Texans formula for success and he illustrates these concepts through stories that span the franchise's history. This is a must-read for anyone wanting to maximize their effectiveness as a leader.

Blessed to know you and count you among my friends.

**Jim Nantz**
**Emmy Award Winning Broadcaster**

Jamey Rootes has been a remarkable success in leading corporations and sports teams to higher levels of achievement. *The Winning Game Plan* is an invaluable handbook for anyone looking to improve their leadership skills and be more productive.

**Leigh Steinberg**
**CEO, Steinberg Sports and Entertainment**

★★★★★

As one of the premier leaders in the world of sports and business today, Jamey Rootes has given us an inside look at his leadership style. This is a must-read for anyone looking to learn and grow.

**Mark Mastrov**
**Founder, 24 Hour Fitness**

Jamey and his team have been terrific partners with the Southeastern Conference through the Texas Bowl. Because of this relationship, I have had the good fortune of witnessing firsthand the positive impact of the many principles Jamey thoughtfully presents in *The Winning Game Plan*. He has surrounded himself with a terrific team, built a winning culture, and keeps everyone focused on a compelling purpose. Building and maintaining these three essential elements comprise the majority of his focus and as a result his organization consistently delivers outstanding outcomes. His book clearly lays out his winning approach and provides valuable lessons for leaders at all levels.

**Greg Sankey**
**Commissioner, Southeastern Conference**

Jamey Rootes has always been a leader; a leader of people and of industry. His energy, vision, empathy, kindness, and intellect have drawn people to him throughout his career. In the business of sports, he's widely respected as one of the sharpest minds and executives in team sports, and he's had success every step of the way.

His leadership lessons are ones we can all learn from and apply to our daily life.

**Abe Madkour**
**Publisher,** *Sports Business Journal*

★★★★★

In *The Winning Game Plan,* Jamey Rootes captures the essence of team building: Valuing colleagues, mentoring associates, and influencing internal and external constituencies to yield the fabric of winning organizations. Jamey draws upon his rich and diverse background in sports, his experiences in a variety of leadership positions, and his enormous ability to lead through wildly divergent challenges to produce concepts that can be applied in any walk of life. This book describes proven principles to find the best in people and to inspire them to collaborations and successes unattainable by individuals alone.

Our organization has enjoyed a long and successful partnership with Jamey, the Texans, and NRG Stadium and I can attest that *The Winning Game Plan* not only is a worthwhile addition to any leader's library, but it represents exactly the manner in which Jamey Rootes has lived his life and managed his career.

**Bob Bowlsby**
**Commissioner, Big 12 Conference**

★★★★★

I am proud to claim Jamey as an alumnus of Clemson University. He is exactly the type of leader we hope all our students will go on to become—a servant-leader who strives every day to make a difference for others and to make the world a better place. From his days as our student body president and a leader on our two-time National Championship soccer team, to his success as one of the top executives in the world of professional sports, he has been a truly visionary leader who always has a plan to win. I am glad Jamey is sharing his winning game plan, as well as his valuable insight and experience, with the world in his new book.

**Jim Clements, Ph.D.**
**President, Clemson University**

When Houston Texans founder Bob McNair told me in 2000 he was going to "think outside the box" and hire a "soccer guy" to guide his sales and marketing department, I privately questioned McNair's ability to head an NFL expansion franchise. A soccer guy making NFL business decisions? What kind of move would that turn out to be? It turned out to be a shrewd move by McNair.

Hiring Jamey Rootes, president and general manager of Major League Soccer's Columbus Crew, was one of the smartest business decisions McNair ever made. Over the last twenty-one years, including the last sixteen as the Texans President, Jamey has rewarded the McNair family's faith in him. He oversees a business operation that's made the franchise one of the most successful in professional sports.

Shortly after Jamey was hired, McNair introduced us, and I was immediately impressed with his energy and his enthusiasm about taking on such an enormous project—building the business side of an NFL expansion franchise.

Jamey was highly recommended to McNair by Kansas City Chiefs owner Lamar Hunt, also the owner of the Columbus Crew. Hunt's recommendation was gold in professional sports, and McNair's trust in Hunt put Jamey in position to develop an NFL business side in his vision. He's proved a hundred times over the trust Hunt and McNair showed in him was richly deserved.

So many things have impressed me about Jamey over the last two decades. Perhaps most impressive is he's a 24/7 workaholic who finds time to be a devoted husband and father who is also heavily involved in the Houston community.

Other things about Jamey that have impressed me are his dedication to his job and his loyalty to the McNair family; the pride he takes in the success of his organization; and the trust his employees, or "teammates" as he calls them, have for him. He's a dynamic leader and a tireless worker whose exuberance inspires those who work with him and for him.

And last, but certainly not least, is somehow Jamey Rootes has found the time and energy to write an informative, insightful, and entertaining book, *The Winning Game Plan*, a blueprint for starting and running a successful sports organization that's deeply rooted in its community.

**John McClain**
**Sportswriter, *Houston Chronicle***

In business and in life, it is invaluable to have a short list of go-to friends and colleagues to call on for wisdom and honest dialogue. I am blessed to have Jamey Rootes on my short list. If you are looking to break into the sports business, or looking to gain insights to apply to your organization, this book provides a rare glimpse into the NFL and one of its most respected clubs.

**Greg Beadles**
**Executive Vice President, Atlanta Falcons Football Club**

*The Winning Game Plan* is a powerful and passionate roadmap that helps a leader discern when to make principled decisions versus business decisions. Knowing the difference, and when to apply either approach, can save a business's future.

Well done, Jamey! In *The Winning Game Plan*, you've organically captured the trait that defines leadership in a super-crisis. Everyone is wounded in a super-crisis. Empathy, creativity, and vision are the watchwords when the cheering seems to stop. More of this please!

**Spencer Tillman**
**Husband, Father, Thought-Leader, Entrepreneur, and**
**Network Broadcaster**

*The Winning Game Plan* is a leadership "how to" and so much more. For those of us who have known Jamey since he arrived in Houston twenty years ago, this book describes the incredible success he has had establishing the Houston Texans into a great sports franchise. Jamey is both a student of leadership theory and an admirer of great leaders, and he has captured what he's learned in easy-to-digest, memorable vignettes. Along the way, he discusses the challenges, disappointments, and victories he has experienced and how they have shaped his approach to building and leading a purpose-driven team of committed professionals. I learned leadership tips that I can apply every day, and I recommend this book to anyone who hopes to inspire others to accomplish more than they previously thought possible.

**Bob Harvey**
**President and CEO, Greater Houston Partnership**

Jamey Rootes is one of the most inspirational leaders I have ever known. I'll never forget the first time we met. He had invited me to lunch at the Texans' offices, which are located at NRG stadium. I'm not sure what I was expecting, but it wasn't what I got. We had lunch in the cafeteria! There were players in workout gear, coaches, administrative employees, and everyone all the way up to their corporate executives, all in the same place and all on equal status. They were all happy and the energy in that room was infectious. That demonstrated to me one of Jamey's greatest skills, the ability to engage everyone and to make everyone feel they are a critical part of the team. He's genuine, driven, a man of great character and discipline, smart, and just the kind of person everyone wants to be around and wants to work hard for.

Jamey is one of Houston's greatest treasures. His community and philanthropic work with major organizations such as the United Way, leadership with the Greater Houston Partnership, and steadfast commitment to selfless contributions for the Houston community are inspiring. And the success he has delivered with the Houston Texans as one of the top ten most successful professional sports franchises in the world is the ultimate example of his leadership and vision.

**Bob Charlet**
**Market President and Publisher,** *Houston Business Journal*

Jamey Rootes is truly one of the most positive and innovative leaders I've ever been associated with. He has helped build the Texans into a winner, both on and certainly off the field. He has always been able to captivate an audience, and he does just that in this book!

**Andre Ware**
**Heisman Trophy Winner and ESPN Color Analyst**

One of the main reasons the Texans are among the most valuable franchises in the NFL is the endless drive of Jamey Rootes. He's constantly looking to make the gameday experience better and always looking to make each season ticket member, fan, and sponsor feel special and extremely well taken care of. He's relentlessly positive and makes sure everyone on his team shares the same enthusiasm to get better every day.

There might be someone in the sports industry who is more positive, productive, and inspiring than Jamey Rootes, but I haven't met them. His relentless drive to improve, innovate, and create a fantastic experience for the fans, sponsors, and community is infectious. It is no accident how the Texans have sold out every game in franchise history. It's the work of Jamey Rootes and his carefully selected team that shares the same ethic.

**Marc Vandermeer**
**Vice President, Broadcasting and Voice of the Houston Texans**

★★★★★

When asked by leaders of Houston's preeminent development professionals organization to enlist a keynote speaker for our 2019 annual conference, I immediately thought of Jamey Rootes, president of the Houston Texans. I had heard Jamey speak before, so I knew he was a powerful motivator. In addition, the Houston Texans, after demonstrating incredible compassion and support for Houstonians in need after the devastation of Hurricane Harvey in 2017, had again lifted up the city in 2018 with a thrilling nine-game winning streak that earned us the AFC South Championship title. With that as backdrop, along with the significant volunteer leadership roles Jamey had played as chairman of the United Way of Greater Houston and of the Greater Houston Partnership, we were confident that he would do a great job and be a big draw.

On conference day, when the program organizers looked out at the sold-out, standing-room-only crowd of some three hundred fifty participants, we all breathed a sigh of relief. Success, right? A full house! Then, as we listened to Jamey speak, something magical began to happen. First, you could have heard a pin drop in the room (which is extremely rare for a group of development professionals). The participants were leaning in, taking notes, asking thoughtful questions, and setting the mobile conference app abuzz with questions, comments, and shout-outs of thanks and encouragement.

The energy in the room was palpable, fueled by Jamey's proficiency, through stories and examples from his personal experiences, as well as from others he has studied. He boosted our courage and confidence and fortified our belief—as individuals and as a group—in our abilities and in our responsibility to achieve great things. Best of all, Jamey delivered his messages of inspiration from a place of incredible intellect and authenticity, clearly built on a foundation of impeccable values and deeply rooted faith.

Jamey Rootes is not only an outstanding speaker, he is an outstanding thinker and a true student of leadership and leaders—Lamar Hunt and Bob McNair, among many others. Himself, a student class president, an accomplished athlete, sports team captain, and graduate of highest academic achievement at all levels of education, Jamey has something very meaningful and unique to say based on his own significant success as a leader, and he expresses it in an uplifting, practical, and interesting way.

I am truly grateful to Jamey for writing this book. Not only will it assist all those who were frantically trying to take notes when Jamey spoke during our conference to continue learning from Jamey's wisdom and leadership strategies, it also will provide an opportunity for leaders and emerging leaders worldwide to benefit from his teachings. For those who serve in industry, business, education, the faith community, healthcare, law, sports, community service, sales, and all organizations dedicated to engaging others, this book provides guidance and support. Jamey can help all of us who struggle to remain positive, encouraging, and confident to do so successfully during the up seasons, as well as during those seasons when things are not going as well as planned.

Now, every time I walk into NRG Stadium on Houston Texans game day and am greeted warmly by a Houston Texans employee—

who is clearly dedicated to making sure every guest has a positive, memorable experience—I know that this is no accident. This is the result of the leadership and personal inspiration of Jamey Rootes.

In closing, I am reminded of the Chinese proverb, "When the student is ready, the teacher appears." If you are ready to become an even better person than you are now, in order to more fully realize your potential as a human being, as well as to hone your skills in motivating, inspiring, encouraging, and bringing out the best in all those around you, I encourage you to read *The Winning Game Plan*, and welcome Jamey Rootes into your life's journey of learning and leading.

Note: Houston Methodist has been honored to serve as the official healthcare provider of the Houston Texans since the franchise began in 2002.

**Susan Coulter**
**President and CEO, Houston Methodist Hospital Foundation**

# CONTENTS

# Foreword

J amey Rootes is a difference maker. Over a 30-year career in
leadership, which includes heading up two successful major
league sports franchise startups, he has established a reputation
of excellence and innovation. The leader he is today is built upon
the experience he has gained and the steps he has taken to define
and create his own leadership journey. In this book, he shares his
formula for success with you.

Over the seventeen years I have known Jamey, I have often
found myself thinking, "I wonder what it would be like to work for
Jamey Rootes?" As a friend, I've watched him demonstrate a
passion, intensity, and authenticity that draws others to him. His
very presence makes others sit up, lean forward, and listen intently.
In today's business world, being genuine goes a long way towards
building credibility. Jamey has a way of making those around him
feel important and special. And that's what makes others want to
work with him.

At the Houston Texans, hustle does not stop at the sidelines.
Jamey sets the vision for the entire organization, ensuring that the
details of putting on a game are executed with precision. While the
players are on the field, Jamey oversees the business operations and
creates a fan experience that generates both memories and a
powerful home-field advantage for the Texans. His leadership style
and influence are the secret sauce that translate attending a game
into fandom and loyalty. Building that kind of committed following
requires constantly improving the experience for fans and sponsors

through ongoing engagement. That is what Jamey has done for the Texans over the past two decades.

His optimistic attitude permeates his team and inspires them to go beyond their last best to achieve the next great success. He expects a lot from others, but he never asks anything of his team or his partners that he wouldn't do himself. Jamey quotes revered leaders like Vince Lombardi and Don Shula the same way a pastor cites passages from scripture. One of his oft cited quotes, attributed to both musician John Lennon and author Paulo Coelho rings home each time I hear it: "Everything will be okay in the end, and if it's not okay, it's not the end." This speaks to how Jamey combines positive thinking and perseverance to overcome adversity.

Every leader knows that challenges come with the territory. Jamey doesn't back down from any challenge. In 2006, the Texans were approached by the NCAA about taking over the failing Houston Bowl, which was heavily in debt. The game had changed sponsor names more times than a check forger on the run. Jamey agreed to take it over, provided he could re-brand it and rebuild it his way. Thus, the Texas Bowl was born. With his typical zeal and commitment to excellence, Jamey transformed the Texas Bowl into what is now the most successful non-playoff post-season game.

He not only gives his all for his team, he does the same for his community. That is a leadership tenet Jamey adheres to adamantly. Jamey Rootes loves Houston, investing himself into making the city a better place. He is a genuine promoter of his city, and he does so with authenticity and commitment, whether serving as Board Chair for the United Way or leading the Board of Directors for the Greater Houston Partnership. If it's important to the city, chances are you'll see Jamey involved and in the middle of it. In many ways, Houston reflects who Jamey Rootes is and what he has accomplished—

a fertile ground where ideas are built into major businesses that make   a difference. Optimism and belief in what can be is reflected in how Jamey leads. He dreams big and sets a high bar, exceeding expectations in everything he does.

*The Winning Game Plan* offers you practical advice on how to be a more effective leader by adopting the proven methods and processes Jamey has developed and executed over his career. He delivers insight into how he leads and the experience he creates for his team. I believe you'll enjoy the journey, and I know you will come out a better person through his advice. It's the next best thing to being a valued member of Jamey's team.

Enjoy the read.

Scott McClelland
President, HEB Food and Drug

# Introduction

So, you want to be a leader? Leadership can be an incredibly rewarding experience. I have always found it exciting and intellectually stimulating to create systems, processes, and practices that help others achieve exceptional results. I find it especially fun to help teammates become the best version of themselves and realize potential they never knew they had. This isn't easy, but nothing valuable ever is. In fact, the beginning of my leadership journey was a quintessential trial by fire that pushed me to the limit. If not for great mentors, a willingness to work as hard as needed to develop my leadership skills, and some luck, my foray as a leader would have likely ended in flames.

My early goals involved *playing* sports, not *managing* them. When I stepped onto the campus of Clemson University as a freshman in 1984, I had aspirations of becoming a professional soccer player. I had never contemplated a career outside of that, yet as I finished my collegiate career, I learned that the options for talented soccer players in America were essentially nil. So, I toyed with the thought of going into sports management. In the meantime, I took a job in sales at IBM. Their training program was second to none, and I was confident that whatever my next career move would be, knowing how to use a computer would be a necessary skill. It was 1989 and although I was right about the future of computers, I had no idea how the digital revolution would impact practically everything in the world over the next few decades.

After three years at IBM, with amazing mentors like my manager Fred Bentfeld, I knew something was wrong. Something was missing. I needed athletics in my life, but I didn't know if I wanted to be a coach or work in a sports business. I called Bobby Robinson, the athletic director at Clemson, and asked him to lunch. I told Bobby of my quandary, and he said, "Coaching and working in sports management are mutually exclusive. You need to decide between the two." I still wasn't sure which one I wanted most, but what I did know was that the time had come for me to make progress towards something that would fuel my passion for athletics. Back at IBM, the entire company was bracing for its first major downsizing, starting with voluntary separations. While most of my coworkers might have felt the sting of their career aspirations going down the drain, I thought, "Here's my chance! I can exit gracefully and get paid for it." And so, I retired from IBM at the ripe old age of 26.

I packed up my Acura Legend and began a cross-country trip, staying with friends, conducting informational interviews in the sports industry with anyone who would visit with me, and generally having a blast. I ended up in San Diego and considered making it my permanent home. After spending months skiing, mountain biking, and reading like crazy, I applied for a job as a bartender at a beachside dive. In the midst of completing the job application, reality hit me. "What am I doing? This isn't my dream." I needed a new plan. So, I packed up the Acura, said goodbye to my California friends, and headed back to Georgia. My plan was to get an MBA, coach soccer, and work in an athletic department so I could decide once and for all between coaching and sports management. I landed at Indiana University to complete my MBA program. As great as the academic experience was, I still needed to satisfy my need to get back into athletics.

After my second year at IU, I accepted a position in brand management at Procter & Gamble, still hoping to find a sports job. While at Procter & Gamble, I maintained all of the contacts I had made in the sports industry. One day, opportunity came knocking, twice. The first was an invitation to become the global soccer manager for Reebok. The other was to join Major League Soccer in some capacity at some point. That didn't sound very definitive. Kansas City Chiefs owner Lamar Hunt and his group liked me, but the league had yet to be fully formed. I was told to sit tight. While speaking to Tim Connolly of the Chiefs, who was leading the MLS franchise efforts for Lamar, I said boldly, "Well, if you're not ready to make an offer, I'm going to accept the job at Reebok." My comment was met with a slightly panicked look on Tim's face. Just what I was hoping for. "No, don't do that," he said. "Give me an hour and keep an eye on your fax machine." I went back to my desk at the worldwide headquarters of P&G. At exactly the one-hour mark, my fax machine began to hum. I could make out the Kansas City Chiefs helmet, but not much else. When the fax completed printing, I could see that it was an offer to become General Manager of a yet to be determined MLS franchise. My sports leadership adventure had begun!

★★★★★

I was 29 years old when I was hired as General Manager of a startup Major League Soccer franchise that would eventually be named the Columbus Crew. Thanks to the generosity of Lamar Hunt and his family, I had a five-year runway to try things, succeed at times, fail often, and most importantly learn how to be a leader others would follow. That experience nearly did me in and it tested my true commitment to being a leader.

We accomplished many things in Columbus. When I left, we had the largest season ticket base in the league and we completed the first soccer-specific stadium ever for a Major League Soccer franchise. That stadium was named the foremost stadium of the year, not because of its quality, but because it started a wildfire of stadium construction for Major League Soccer franchises. This opportunity in Columbus did not happen by accident. Actually, I don't believe anything important happens by accident. This was the culmination of a five-year quest to break into the sports industry.

By the time I turned 34, I had realized a station in life that could have actually been my final destination. I was running a professional soccer team in my own stadium in a city that I loved. However, I felt like I needed a new challenge. It was October, 1999. In the midst of all this self-reflection, I received a call from a dear friend, Buffy Filippell, one of the first executive recruiters in the professional sports industry. "Hey Jamey, I have an opportunity for you," she said. "I think you're going to like this." I hadn't actually been looking for an opportunity, but I was intrigued. "What do you think about working in the National Football League?" I held the phone to my ear in silence and glanced out of the window of my home in German Village in stunned disbelief. Sure, I had wanted a change, but this was almost unbelievable.

A herd of thoughts ran through my mind before I finally responded, "Ummm, yeah, let me think about it." I hadn't even asked what the position was or with what team. As Buffy rattled off the details, my mind went blank. She explained that a new team was being formed in Houston, Texas. It would replace the vacancy left by the Houston Oilers. A man named Bob McNair had purchased the franchise rights and the team would begin play in 2002. A tingling giddiness rose up inside of me. It was a mixture of excitement and complete shock that I had been approached for a leading management position at an NFL team. Finally, I found my voice.

"Well, that sounds nice, but I need to talk it over with my wife. I'll get back to you." Then, I hung up. Even as the words spilled from my mouth, I realized that using my wife as an excuse to not provide a more definitive response might have sounded a bit like avoidance, but it was the truth. I was still a newlywed, having been married just one year prior. My wife Melissa was happy where we were and we hadn't once discussed building a life outside of Columbus. For five minutes I stared at the phone and thought, "What am I doing!" Finally, I called her back and told her what I had meant to say the first time, "I can't accept the job without my wife's approval, but of course I'm interested in the NFL!" I agreed to head to Houston for a visit after my talk with Melissa.

Surprised only begins to describe my reaction when Melissa expressed her excitement at the opportunity to move to Texas. She was an Ohio native, but she was ready for a change. It turned out to be the perfect move for us. After spending the previous five years launching a professional sports franchise, I now had the chance to do it again. So, together, we traveled to Houston for a visit with the new owner and other stakeholders. The energy was right and the possibilities were endless. There was no doubt that this was the right move and the right time for me to step into this kind of leadership position. I didn't have all the answers. In fact, I didn't even have all the questions. But I believed I had a supportive owner who would allow me the margin to try new approaches, learn as I grew as a leader, and build a world-class organization from the ground up.

For the first thirty months, we put in place all of the foundational components required to successfully compete in the NFL. We built the organization and a beautiful stadium for the team, assembled a robust set of commercial partners, and filled our required base of season ticket members, club seat members, and suite patrons. It was a thrilling and exhausting experience, but it was what was required to set the franchise up for long-term success. During this time, I engaged a consultant to help us more completely flesh out our operating approach. I didn't have all the questions or all the answers. I figured a third-party perspective would help my management team shape up into a well-oiled machine quickly so we could move forward on some of the fresh ideas we were generating. "You know what would help me a lot," he said. "If I could spend some time with each of your direct reports, just to ask a few questions. Nothing too heavy, you know. Just a meeting with each person ought to do it."

His request sounded simple enough. And really, I thought it was a great idea. I'd be interested to find out what he learned during his time with my team. Not that I was using him to spy on anyone. I just wanted his take on who I might watch closely as potential to move up in the ranks as the organization grew. "Sure thing," I said, feeling as if I were exemplifying the open-minded kind of manager I had always admired. What happened would completely transform my leadership philosophy. After finishing interviews with my leadership team, the consultant asked to visit with me late on a Friday afternoon. At the start of our conversation, he said, "You're probably going to want to go home after this." *What?* I braced myself for what I thought would be dismal news about a poorly selected rag-tag group of employees who he thought might need to be retrained or eliminated altogether. To my surprise, his comments didn't focus so much on my team, but on me. During our discussion, he painted a not-so-flattering picture of me as President of the Houston Texans, based on the feedback received from my team. Although I didn't know I had initiated it, I was being provided my first 360-degree feedback session . . . and it hurt.

He captured the true essence of the message by saying, "I'm sure you have heard the phrase 'micromanager,' but there is no such thing as a 'micro-leader.' You are a micromanager, but not yet a leader." Once I got over the initial sting of his assessment, I realized that, despite the many successes I had experienced twice in a startup environment, the skills that had contributed to those successes were not the same skills that would deliver success in the future. In fact, holding onto my comfortable micromanaging habits would eventually lead to my downfall. It was a dramatic paradigm shift that launched me on a leadership development journey that has led to this book.

★★★★★

As you level-up in your leadership trajectory, you're going to have to release some old stuff, even if you think that old stuff is what got you to where you are. Every new leadership opportunity offers new chances to grow and learn. In the words of Marshall Goldsmith, "What got you here won't get you there." Accept that from the start and you'll be well positioned to receive what's next. The new frontier you face—whether leading a new company or department, starting your own enterprise, or flexing your leadership muscles— is a chance to grow as a leader and as a human being.

Your ability to impact results can grow exponentially when you're sitting in the top spot. In fact, my friend, and the imminently respected CEO of Texas Children's Hospital, Mark Wallace says in his leadership maxims, "Leadership always influences or determines outcomes, not some of the time, but all of the time." When you develop the talents of others, you can influence outcomes as well. On the flip side, leadership comes with its own unique set of challenges, and challenges are to be welcomed. They are the impetus for change, learning, and growth. But you *must* learn from the challenges. Follow the guidelines in this playbook and you'll have a reliable set of resources to meet each challenge head-on.

Here, you'll learn a proven approach to leading a business—any business—to exceptional and sustained success. These are the same principles that we have used at the Houston Texans since inception more than twenty years ago. Through trial, error, and adjustment, these guiding principles have helped us deliver breakthrough financial results for our partners, a rewarding workplace experience for our teammates, tremendous customer loyalty, and a reputation as a committed caretaker of our community. Throughout this book you will notice that I often use acronyms to describe important concepts. This is both purposeful and powerful. At the end of the book, you'll learn how to leverage this technique. For now, just embrace getting to know these principles through stories that have dramatically impacted my life.

I hope this book helps you make progress towards becoming the leader you want to be. To see that growth, you'll have to embrace the reality that you don't know everything . . . and you never will. I trust that you are ready to be better and to influence others to do the same. Most of all, take away some tools and techniques to become your best self as a leader. Enjoy!

# CHAPTER 1

# Are You a Manager or a Leader?

O ften, the concepts of leadership and management are used interchangeably. Getting them confused is a common misunderstanding, which I learned quite well following my disastrous 360-degree feedback session. I had arrived at my new position as President of the Houston Texans, stepping into an honored leadership position, but with a management mindset.

Management is a function designated by an organization. The "powers that be" designate someone as competent to manage certain aspects within the business. Managers are indeed essential to the company's overall success, but they are not leaders. Leadership is a designation given by followers. Those who understand and effectively communicate the purpose and passion of an organization, who exude knowledge and confidence in the organization's ability to do what needs to be done collectively, who know the overarching goals and outcomes desired, and who inspire others to be and do their best are designated as leaders by those who look to them for direction. Leadership and management are on opposite ends of the spectrum. A good friend and successful entrepreneur, Debra Myers once explained the difference this way: "You can't work *on* your business while you're working *in* your business." Managers work *in* the business while leaders work *on* the business. Managers focus on the individual. Great managers understand the talents, weaknesses, and mentality of their individual employees and they use this to enable exceptional performance. Many coaches are very skilled managers and they are fixated on putting their players in the best position to help the team win.

Leaders, by contrast, work *on* the business and focus on the collective. Leaders work with their followers—what I call teammates—to define an inspiring vision that the entire team wants to realize. They keep everyone's eyes focused on that objective. Leaders are authentic about their passion to achieve the vision of the organization, and they over-communicate it to create absolute clarity. Leaders inspire a shared vision. Once that vision is established it becomes a powerful tool. From there, communication becomes critical. To distinguish yourself as a great leader of a collective, rather than a manager of individuals, you have to walk the walk and show that you are all in, for the organization, for your teammates, and for the community you impact. When you do, you inspire others to do the same.

Lamar Hunt, owner of the Columbus Crew, was the epitome of walking the walk.

On a particular game day during my tenure as president of the team, I led a pre-game briefing attended by the majority of our staff. As we gathered in a tented structure outside the stadium that served as our stadium club, my team was facing me as I addressed them. Just beyond the group, I could see Lamar Hunt walking down the sidewalk adjacent to the stadium. Suddenly, he halted his casual stroll, bent down, and picked up a piece of trash that was on the ground, then put it into the nearby trash can. I told my staff to turn around and look at the owner of our team picking up trash. I made the point, "If he can do it, we all must do it." I'm not sure if Lamar did that on purpose, but his example did more to reinforce the importance of maintaining a clean stadium than any number of speeches could ever do.

Leaders need to be involved with some of the activities that lead to their organization's success, adding their oversight to ensure that everything is being taken care of—working *in* the business. But that can't come at the expense of the responsibilities that ensure long-term, sustained success—working *on* the business. The more time you spend working *in* the business, the more likely you are to micromanage people and activities. I call this leading by command and control. Here, you give specific orders that subordinates are to act on without question or improvisation. The focus is on the inputs rather than the outcomes. With this approach, not only do you risk frustrating your teammates, you limit the organization's performance because you are not using your high-level skills effectively. Working *on* the business is the key to unleashing your organization's full potential. This is what allows you to move from leading by command control to leading by remote control.

When you lead by remote control, you establish a set of expected outcomes within a specific time frame and leave the required inputs up to the discretion of your teammates. Once you establish a clear, mutually agreeable vision of success, and commit the necessary resources and support, the outcome happens naturally, without your active involvement or direct oversight. You are now free to resume the important job of working on your business.

To illustrate the pull created by clearly establishing expected outcomes, consider the game of football. Why do teams try to get the ball in the end zone? Before the game started, both teams agreed that getting the ball into the end zone would result in six points for the scoring team. Given that the goal is to score the most points, teams develop strategies to move the ball into their opponent's end zone. There are any number of ways to do this. The method is irrelevant as long as the rules of the game are respected. The same is true when you manage by remote control. You create a game that your teammates play autonomously. As their leader, you serve as the referee and scorekeeper. More often than not, the game becomes the teacher by the positive and negative reinforcement that naturally results from each action taken.

To begin your journey towards managing by remote control, implement what I call the S.O.F.T. technique.

## Strengths

Like a coach, one of your responsibilities as a leader is to identify the strengths of each player and identify a role that allows these strengths to be best utilized for the benefit of the team.

## Outcomes

Rather than define activities or actions for each teammate, clearly define the right outcomes for their role. What does a win look like? Once that is established, leave it up to them to figure out how to get that done within the timeframe allotted. When setting outcomes, you can be either descriptive or prescriptive. Being descriptive establishes a challenge to be overcome or an opportunity to exploit. Being prescriptive provides a solution. Whenever possible, be descriptive, not prescriptive.

When you are adequately descriptive regarding your expectations, you paint a clear picture of success that can be realized in many different ways. You articulate *what* you want accomplished without much concern for how it is achieved, as long as it is honest, ethical, efficient, and accurate. In contrast, *prescribing* a formula to

16

be followed focuses on how—the steps that may or may not lead to a desired outcome. More importantly, a prescriptive approach invites execution risk. When your teammates simply follow orders they are not nearly as motivated to follow their own path to the result. Leading by remote control requires an intense focus on outcomes, not inputs. If you have ever heard someone say after a failure, "Well, I followed your instructions," you know firsthand the pitfalls of a prescriptive approach. Be descriptive to unleash the full potential of your team.

## Fit

Supporting your team and giving them opportunities to fail, to learn, and to get better is important. However, at some point, you must determine if each team member is still a good fit for the role or for the organization. Begin evaluating team members, particularly those who are struggling, by asking: Does this team member need a specific performance plan? Is it time to make a change?

I learned the importance of fit from our cheer director several years back. She approached me with the decision to replace a member of the cheer squad and I gave her some push back. I knew the young lady in passing and she seemed quite professional, so I questioned the decision to remove her. Our cheer director replied, "Keeping the wrong people on the bus is unfair to all the right people." I couldn't argue with that. When examining a teammate's fit, you can't focus only on the individual. You have to consider their impact on the team. In Texas, this is known as the "cockroach effect." It's not what they eat, it's what they spoil.

## Talent

Perhaps the most important job of a leader is to find the right talent for the team. Your talent creates the ceiling for your performance. You must get this one right. According to the 2019 Predictive Index survey of 156 CEOs, finding the right talent is the number one challenge keeping leaders up at night. Talent concerns are at the heart of four of their top five issues. So, how do you attract the right talent? There are many tactics that you can follow to *push* talent towards your business, but the following two key items will actually *pull* the best and brightest to your doorstep.

1. **Create a winning culture**. Strong, positive cultures are the preferred destination of top talent. When you have a great culture, your employees are not merely satisfied, they are loyal and they become champions and ambassadors for your organization.

2. **Build a great workplace.** Attracting and keeping great employees requires you to build a great place to work. Ask your employees what they want and give it to them. Further, become recognized as a great place to work and build a reputation for it. It's not hard, but it does take some resources. More importantly, it takes commitment and an enlightened understanding that your most important assets walk out the door of your organization every night. Everyone is a free agent.

Following the S.O.F.T. approach, especially taking the time to clearly define and gain alignment on the right outcomes, allows you to take your hands off the wheel and give teammates the opportunity to take control and be fully accountable. From there, you can check in periodically with one-on-ones to ask questions, provide support and resources, and manage by remote control.

# Leaders Communicate Purpose with Passion

Now that you're walking the walk as a leader, you've got to talk the talk. Essentially, you're communicating, or really, over-communicating. The ability to communicate clearly and persuasively is key to any leader's success. Communication is not merely what is spoken or written. Leadership-level communication has a much higher standard than that. For leaders, communication is what is heard, remembered, and acted upon.

Communicating in a manner that is clear, inspiring, and persuasive is the most important leadership tool at your disposal. *What* you communicate to your teammates is equally—if not more—important as *how* you communicate. As a leader, you are a guide. You're the north star, the insider people look to for vision, inspiration, and clarification of the all-encompassing reason the entire organization exists. You must communicate that to your team with a passion so energetic and contagious they inspire others to contribute elective effort. Communicating a clear and compelling purpose is the key to evoking passion among your teammates. The word "passion" comes from the Latin word "pati" which means the willingness to suffer and sacrifice for what you hold dear. With true pati, you love something so much that you will do just about anything for it. That's the type of commitment you want your purpose to create. Therefore, the goal is to have a purpose that engenders passion.

As an organization, the Houston Texans have three imperatives which encapsulate the purpose of the organization:

1. Win championships
2. Create memorable experiences
3. Do great things for Houston

Winning championships sounds simple, but in the NFL it is anything but. The league is designed with rules to create competitive parity and drive every team, over time, to eight wins and eight losses. The maniacal commitment to parity drives intense fan interest and business success. Fortunately, our first imperative could be more accurately described as being fully committed to winning a championship. The games are tightly contested, injuries can eliminate a team's chances, even the ball is shaped to promote unpredictability. The bottom line is, we must always conduct ourselves in a manner that leaves no room for doubt in the minds of our fans that we are 100 percent committed to, and passionate about our purpose of winning championships.

Some might think that people travel to NRG Stadium—home of the Texans—on Sundays in the fall just to watch a football game. I'll let you in on a little secret: Fans can watch all of our games for free at home on TV. The truth is that our fans make their way to NRG every Sunday for something more. They come for memorable experiences. For them, game day is a bonding experience like no other, from tailgating to the rituals and traditions they participate in throughout the game. The passion comes through with each interaction a fan has with our organization. Game day is a chance for them to participate with the action on the field, which is something they just can't get at home. Game day at the stadium is not just a football game for us or our fans. It's The Texans Experience. It's a chance to stand shoulder to shoulder and be part of our home field advantage. The visitors know they aren't playing against just forty-eight football players today. They are taking on 71,500 screaming, face-painted Texans! Houston is one of the most diverse cities in America, and nothing brings us together like the game of football. Monday to Saturday, we live as individuals, but on Sunday, we come together as one. We are Texans.

Our ability to create memorable experiences touches fans young and old, from all backgrounds, and at so many levels. When Texans fan Sebastián Muñoz brought his son to a game, the experience made a lasting impression on them both.

*"My son, Tristan, who is 7 years old, and I have been loyal Houston Texans fans since the beginning and have loved every moment that we experience watching the games," Muñoz wrote in a letter. "Recently, we attended our first game together. As the team was walking off the field, my son kept telling me that he couldn't believe we were there at the game watching our team. As we stood at the edge of the sitting area near the 10-yard line, one of the players handed his receiver gloves to an usher and pointed at my son. Tristan then looked at me in disbelief and said, 'Dad, he saw me! Dad, he saw me!' As the usher walked to our location, he handed my son the receiver's gloves. To see my son's face covered with joy and excitement was unbelievable. That was a moment I will never forget, nor will Tristan. I would like to thank you for giving my son an experience he will never forget."*

Our avenues for doing great things for Houston are many and varied. We provide massive visibility for our city and generate hundreds of millions of dollars in economic impact annually. We have brought two Super Bowls to Houston and have helped our city become one of America's leading soccer markets. Since 2006, we have managed Houston's collegiate bowl game, which is now the fifth best attended bowl game in America. We are champions for youth, serve the military, honor first responders, and serve Houston in so many other ways. We have donated roughly $36 million to charity, and we are regularly the number one donor to the United Way, per capita. In times of crisis, we always have Houston's back. We have taken the concept of community support, which is basically a universal endeavor in business, and elevated it to a guiding principle for making decisions as a core component of our reason to be as a franchise. This community commitment is a point of immense pride and a source of inspiration that creates tremendous loyalty among our employees, customers, and fans.

As a football team with lots of resources, visibility, and support, some aspects of exemplifying our purpose with passion might seem easier for us than for other organizations. However, with some creative thought, most organizations can construct a compelling purpose that elicits "pati." To bring pati to life, make sure your entire team understands the overall purpose of the company. Everyone needs to be on the same page. You can't have one department thinking the company's purpose is one thing, another group assuming the purpose is something else, and yet another that articulates the purpose in an entirely different way. That won't work. Here's a story to illustrate what that looks like: A man approaches a group of laborers. He asks the first laborer, "What are you doing?" The man replies, "I'm laying bricks." He asks the same question of a second man, who says, "I'm building a wall." The man walks up to a third laborer and asks, "What are you doing?" This laborer replies, "I'm creating a cathedral where families can come together and celebrate the Lord."

Organizations that operate with passion come in all sizes and exist in every business sector. They understand that the drive to succeed at a stated purpose takes passion at all levels of the organization. Here are some companies that get the value of passion:

Kellogg doesn't sell cereal. Rather, they are "Nourishing families so they can flourish and thrive."

ING doesn't engage in financial planning. Instead, they are "Empowering people to stay a step ahead in life and business."

IAG isn't selling life insurance. What they're really doing is "Helping people manage risk and recover from the hardship of unexpected loss."

Motivation fuels your organization's reason for being. What are you doing to help others? Why are you doing that specific thing and not something else? What more can you do with the resources you have? What result would you like to see from your efforts? The answers to these questions and others clarify your purpose and inspire your team and your organization to great heights. When each member of your team knows they make an impact on others through their service, your organization wins. As Gandhi said, "The way to find yourself is to lose yourself in the service of others." Service is good for your soul and it is good for business.

Having a clear and compelling purpose is the key to eliciting "elective effort" from your teammates. Elective effort is the extra mile, the volunteerism, and the mentality that causes teammates to keep going until they get it right. It permeates throughout your organization when people authentically adopt the purpose. Great leaders work hard to inspire elective effort. "Leadership is getting people to do what they don't want to do, in order to get what they do want to get." Those are the words of five-time NFC title winner and two-time Super Bowl winning coach of the Dallas Cowboys, Tom Landry. Leaders communicate a clear and compelling purpose and point everyone's sights there when times are tough. Nobody wants to run wind sprints, but they do want to win on Sunday. Establish a purpose that inspires your team to focus on greatness, rather than the blood, sweat, and tears required to make it happen. Even when they consider the actions needed to reach greatness, find a way to turn those actions into a ceremonial custom. In essence, a ritual.

Rituals are vital in the workplace. They connect employees to the organization and to each other. We have many rituals within the Houston Texans, among them are our annual and season kick-off meetings. These meetings began twenty years ago as the typical, boring presentation of strategy and tactics. Over time, they have become part business meeting and part entertainment extravaganza. Part of the entertainment value of these meetings is that each intern class creates a video and tries to make it the most memorable ever. Each presenting team is challenged to deliver on the three Ns—engage, inform, and inspire—judged by the reaction of the entire organization, which makes up the audience at the meeting. Consequently, each meeting is like a rollicking episode of *Saturday Night Live*, full of laughs, gaffes, and connection.

At one breakfast meeting attended by more than a hundred people in our team auditorium, we had planned a big surprise. Once everyone had gotten a cup of coffee and brought it with them into the auditorium, the show began. The surprise was that our mascot TORO and our cheerleaders would kick off the meeting from the stage. They decided the best way to do this was with a T-shirt toss. So, with music blaring and T-shirts soaring through the air, the coffee cups began flying in tandem. Essentially, we had created a red hot mess. Not the best start for a business meeting, but we laughed until we cried, and realized we had actually delivered on one of our stated organizational imperatives—create memorable experiences. These shared experiences connect people on a deep and human level and are the essence of a great employee experience that creates loyalty.

The connections fans have to live sporting events are partially due to the rituals that exist there, too. You can watch a game on TV, but you miss the rich traditions that play out in the stadium. Some of these are entirely organic and others are encouraged and then adopted by the fan base. One early tradition of the Houston Texans was The Bullpen. We had secured roughly sixty thousand season ticket members and were beginning to place them in the stadium. We knew there was a group of intensely passionate fans who wanted to stand the entire game, paint their faces, and prove to the world that they were the most loyal football fans on the planet. We also knew there was a much larger group that would like to see these fans, but definitely not want to sit among them. Our solution: The Bullpen, which consisted of several sections of seats in the lower level at the north end zone where body painted, fire-eyed, towel-waving fans could yell at the top of their lungs without disturbing the more subtle ticket holders. Fans could decide whether to either sit in The Bullpen or avoid that area at all costs. It was a brilliant way to create a collection of like-minded fans who have been a mainstay of the Houston Texans game day experience since inception.

Traditions bind people together as much as rituals do. But, in the early days, the Texans had no traditions. Because we were an expansion team, we needed our fans to get to know us and to help us create meaningful practices that would become engrained as part of the Texans culture. To do this, we borrowed a tradition from Bayer Leverkusen, a top-tier football club of the German Bundesliga professional football league. We asked our PA announcer to say the first name of each player as they were introduced, and allow the fans to respond with the player's last name. When I reviewed this with our TV crew during a pre-production meeting, they looked at me as if I had two heads. They didn't follow the logic of how this small action would get the fans pumped up and participating in the game as if they were on the field themselves. Despite the reluctance of our TV crew, we pushed on with the idea. Two decades later, this is one of the most recognized and widely adopted fan participation traditions in the National Football League. In fact, last season, the San Francisco 49ers asked their fans to suggest a new tradition for the team to adopt. Their choice? Shouting the last name of the players during introductions.

## Leaders Communicate Values

Communicating values clearly is paramount. Values cannot just be presented as compelling statements on the wall. You have to drive values into the minds and hearts of your team. Only then will you influence behaviors day to day. English essayist, playwright, and poet Samuel Johnson said, "People need to be reminded more often than they need to be instructed." Therefore, you need a constant stream of reminders to influence behavior. Using examples is a powerful reminder of the values, attitudes, actions, and expectations you communicate to your team.

In his book *The Four Obsessions of an Extraordinary Executive*, Patrick Lencioni's third discipline is to "OVER-communicate organizational clarity." *Over*-communicating will likely impact you the same way it will impact your teammates. When you communicate an objective or belief over and over, you get tired of hearing yourself say it, but the repetition reinforces the belief in your mind. Consequently, by the time you have gotten sick and tired of saying the same thing, your team is just beginning to understand what you mean and how they can apply it. In business, repetitive communication of the fundamentals—values, operating philosophy, etc.—is a key to effective leadership and it is an important way leaders create value.

Like most leaders, I wasn't born into the leadership spot. I had to grow into it. Before earning the lead post for the Houston Texans, I paid my dues and learned the ropes at two top global corporations, IBM (sales) and Procter & Gamble (brand management). During those years, I learned a lot about leadership, how it works, what doesn't go over well, how to screw up, and what successful leadership looks like. I came to understand that effective leadership doesn't happen in a silo. There is an obvious four-dimensional reality of leadership that cannot be ignored. Effective leaders recognize each dimension and understand they combine to maximize their influence and potential. Here's how it works:

**Lead Up:** Everybody's got a boss. Even the President of the United States can be "fired" by the voters. Leading up well is how you build trust with whomever holds the top spot above you, whether your board of directors, the owner of your company, or someone else. When you demonstrate that you are a capable, responsible, dependable, and loyal steward, you establish trust with those above you. At the same time, you provide an example of how your teammates should relate to you. Over time, leading up will allow you greater latitude and autonomy, and it shields your direct reports from distractions. Your team is counting on you to lead up well. It's a job only you can do.

**Lead Down:** Your teammates need many things from you, but most importantly, they need clarity. Clearly communicating your expectations enables your teammates to get into flow. Flow is a psychological state of complete immersion in the moment, free of doubt, allowing a dramatic boost in creativity and productivity. When leading down, be clear about available resources and assistance, degrees of latitude for decision making, and other essential elements of success. Equally important is to be decisive when managing down. A clear and decisive plan that is well executed results in consistent success.

**Lead Out:** You and your organization should strive to be respected within the community you serve, and geographically where your business is located. That respect should reflect your competence, integrity, and character. Gaining this respect requires you and your team to reach beyond the walls of the building in which you work and into the organizations, institutions, and facilities that support the community around you. You might sit on a board, donate to a charity, or be the bridge that connects critical resources to a community. As a leader, you must get out, and when you do, the goal is to garner respect. How others outside of your organization perceive you dramatically influences their beliefs about the organization you represent.

**Lead Across:** Build a reputation as an effective collaborator and a great teammate across all areas of your organization. The higher you go, the more friends you will need to get things done. You can constantly build valuable allies by being a teammate others can count on for support and encouragement.

Excelling in only one or two dimensions of four-dimensional leadership is not sustainable, especially as you ascend to the highest levels of an organization. The failure to build your capabilities along all four can be disastrous. If you are already a capable four-dimensional leader, you can always get better. To be the best leadership version of yourself, make four-dimensional leadership an ongoing personal development priority.

# The P.O.W.E.R. of Emotional Intelligence

Ask any self-proclaimed "self-aware" person and they'll swear they have complete control of their emotions at all times. My guess is, that's probably not true. But don't take my word for it. Just observe how they react or respond under pressure, how they treat others in a tense situation, how they behave when things go wrong, or what they say when obstacles seem insurmountable. Understanding how your emotions impact every aspect of your life, being aware of your emotions, and managing them intentionally, consciously, and consistently is what emotional intelligence is all about. It sounds simple, but it takes practice.

The concept of EQ is pretty basic. The human brain has not evolved much since the days when we were constantly at risk of being eaten by a saber-toothed tiger. We have a hard-wired fight-or-flight response from a time when one of our most pressing questions, intended as a means of protection was, "Do I eat this, or does it eat me?" In modern society, particularly in business, that survival mentality can cause huge problems. When the fight-or-flight response is triggered, we have what is called an amygdala hijack. If the level of negative emotion (fear, anger, etc.) rises to a certain level, the rational, thinking part of the brain is turned off and we are only capable of an emotional or irrational response. Not bad when a T-Rex is staring you down on the plains, but terrible when investors are staring you down in the board room. It takes intelligence to make smart leadership decisions. With the power of emotional intelligence, your decision-making skills go through the roof.

The intelligence quotient, or IQ, is the generally accepted measurement of human cognitive ability. Some careers require high IQs, like scientists, engineers, and doctors. Leadership, by contrast, is much more dependent on emotional intelligence, or EQ. IQ is hardwired and measured by an intelligence test. It is inflexible. What you're born with is what you have. EQ, on the other hand, is flexible. It can be increased through disciplined practice. Don't get me wrong, leaders need to have a moderate degree of IQ, but at a certain point, any more is just wasted potential. An abundance of EQ, however, is how leaders get results through others, which is the essence of leadership. The higher you rise in an organizational structure, the less you do *things* and the more you do *people*.

For over two decades, Daniel Goleman has been at the forefront of the concept of emotional intelligence. According to Goleman, EQ determines roughly 80 percent of success in life. Yes, you read that right, 80 percent! Harnessing the P.O.W.E.R. of emotional intelligence helps you keep EQ top of mind and reminds you to constantly elevate your EQ as you become a more effective leader. Here's how the P.O.W.E.R. of emotional intelligence works:

## Personal

The first step towards harnessing the immense power of your natural instincts is to become aware of your emotions. You have to gain control of your emotions, or they will control you and limit your potential.

## Ownership

Own your emotions so they can become productive (and not destructive) for you. Journaling is an effective tool to help you understand your emotions. When faced with a situation that unproductively elevates your emotional state, write it down and work to identify the emotional triggers that drive you. Explore the external factors that impacted your emotional state. Over time, you will get better at identifying what enables your fight-or-flight response. At that point, you are empowered to move on and do something about it.

## Winner

Channel your emotions in a positive fashion to enable winning interactions with others. When you understand the external influences that push your buttons, you recognize them, anticipate their potential impact on your emotion level, and respond with considerably less emotion, thus remaining in calm, rational, and logical. Now you are starting to get results with and through others.

## Empathy

Make a conscious and continuous effort to understand and empathize with the emotions of others. Resist the urge to expect others to view a situation through the same lens you do. Instead, take a step back, listen and, when possible, share the feelings of others. In this way, you demonstrate that you are a leader who values and respects the emotions of others.

## Relate

Closely tied to empathy, relating to others requires you to understand your own emotions and the emotions of others. In this case, your objective is to exert influence in the pursuit of win-win outcomes. Do not mistake this for manipulation or anything less than authentic. Instead, think of this point as the subtle, honest close to any deal—whether you wind up on top or not—demonstrating that you identify with the other person (or their position) in a way that suggests your confidence in a beneficial outcome for all sides.

Managing emotional intelligence is essential in your leadership journey. This, like many other critical concepts, is one to practice throughout your career. You will constantly be faced with new opportunities to use your P.O.W.E.R. for the best outcomes for your organization and your team. Each conversation, each negotiation, each interview or speech is a platform for growing your EQ. Be aware. Be persistent. Be committed to doing better than you did the last time. This is how you build your EQ P.O.W.E.R. A healthy EQ allows leaders to have both a sense of calm in times of crisis and a sense of humor to smooth over situations that might seem uncomfortable for others.

During one particularly tense negotiating session, I uncharacteristically exploded verbally and ended the meeting, demanding that my team get their things and leave. As we walked down the hallway, a safe distance from the rest of the group, one of my teammates said, "Wow, are you okay?"

I replied, "Of course. They were mistaking our kindness for weakness. I just wanted to do a reset. Believe me, they'll call requesting another meeting and they'll come to that meeting with the appropriate mindset." They did call, we did meet, and we did consummate the deal on terms that were good for all of us. Once you have the P.O.W.E.R. of emotional intelligence on your side, you can use your emotions—even anger—to get winning results.

There were so many things I appreciated about Houston Texans founder Bob McNair, but at the top of the list was his ability to navigate even the most contentious situation with incredible grace and humor. I attribute this to his high degree of emotional intelligence. Soon after we launched the Houston Texans, we had a conference call with a group of bankers who were considering whether to finance the team's operations. Our general manager, Charley Casserly, provided an update on the football team and I covered the progress we had made relative to our business. Once we were done, the moderator on the call instructed the bankers, "If you have questions for the management team, please press one."

A few seconds passed as the phone line fell silent. There wasn't even the sound of breathing, which only added to the tension. And then, Bob chimed in robustly, saying, "If you would like to wire your money now, please press two." Everyone had a good laugh, and it was a great example of how humor can navigate the emotions of a tense situation. Bob always had a knack for that and it was one reason why he was a great leader.

In times of crisis, a healthy EQ is an invaluable tool to keep calm and lead your teammates to an optimal outcome. Over the last twenty years, I have had the blessing and the curse of leading the Houston Texans through numerous crisis situations. We have survived hurricanes, floods, and even the first seven months of a global pandemic. Each time, the P.O.W.E.R. of my EQ became the guidepost to help my teammates get through the crisis unscathed and help me maintain my sanity.

In the fall of 2017, I packed for a trip to New Orleans to play the Saints for week three of the pre-season. We had a conference call on

Friday afternoon with our long-time TV partner, ABC-13, to discuss a storm that was developing in the Gulf of Mexico and the impact it could have on our Saturday night telecast. We determined that the storm would miss Houston and we gave the green light for a broadcast as scheduled. I arrived at the Mercedes-Benz Superdome and made my normal laps around the field to shake hands and benchmark things (my term for seeking good ideas to steal) without a care in the world. Man, how plans change. As boxer Mike Tyson once said, "Everyone has a plan until they get punched in the mouth."

As I sat in our suite mid-way through the second quarter, I got a text from Henry Florsheim, president and general manager of KTRK ABC-13, which read, "YOU HAVE TO SEE THIS!" He had forwarded me an internal update from meteorologist Tim Heller indicating that Hurricane Harvey, the mother of all storms with a projected five feet of rain, was coming directly to Houston! This would be a huge threat to the safety and economic viability of the Houston region. We finished the game, then contemplated our next steps field-side. Houston was completely flooded and the damage was expected to get worse. We decided to take the team to Dallas, then determine our next move from there.

Having arrived at the hotel at 4:00 a.m., I tried to get some sleep, but at 6:00 a.m., my friend Pete Derzis from ESPN called. "Hey, we have a sold-out Texas Kickoff game, LSU versus BYU next Saturday. What are we going to do?"

I groggily replied, "The first thing I'm going to do is make some coffee. I'll call you back in ten minutes."

Over the next few days, we moved the Texas Kickoff game to New Orleans, refunding every ticket sold in Houston and selling more than fifty thousand new seats for the relocated game. We also cancelled our Thursday night game in Houston with the Dallas Cowboys, refunding seventy thousand tickets and moved the game to Dallas, selling fifty thousand seats before we cancelled that game and refunded those tickets as well. In total, we sold a hundred thousand tickets in just a few days, but we refunded two hundred thousand tickets. That math just doesn't work.

Our team maintained calm, poise, and focus throughout the entire ordeal. We communicated well, made good decisions based on the facts available at the time, and kept going forward. We cared for our employees and established a $100,000 employee assistance fund that covered hurricane damage inflicted on all our teammates. We saw the "whatever it takes" attitude of our teammates as they stepped up time and again to make sure this crisis would not have the final word. Lastly, our team, the league, and other clubs (and most importantly, J.J. Watt, our future Hall of Fame defensive end) championed flood relief and recovery fundraising that totaled over $60 million to support impacted families along the Gulf Coast, especially those in the Houston area. For me, this entire ordeal turned a two-day road trip into a ten-day adventure from Houston to New Orleans to Dallas to New Orleans and finally back to Houston. Despite the drama, the financial loss, and the devastation to our beloved Houston, it was one of the most rewarding experiences of my career.

What I learned is that once a crisis begins, it's too late to prepare for it. The true nature of your leadership is revealed in times of crisis. Fortunately, we had the right people in the right positions, with a clear and compelling purpose and a powerful culture to drive us forward. Within a crisis is when your fortitude as a leader shines. Pursuing your purpose with passion, living your values, and tapping into your emotional intelligence guides you through almost any challenge.

# CHAPTER 2

# Get the Right People on Your Team

Legendary Florida State University football coach, Bobby Bowden knew the value of having not only the best players on the team, but the right players with the right talent in the right positions. "The guy with the best players usually wins," Bowden would say. The truth of that statement reminds me that you will never outperform the quality of your talent base. This is true on the gridiron and it is true in business.

Getting and keeping the right people on your team is like being a gardener. Those with a green thumb identify the plants that develop well and provide them with water and fertilizer to help them grow to full potential. Likewise, when growing an efficient team, you must quickly identify your stars and ensure they have the right opportunities, compensation, and other requirements to keep them excited about the organization. To keep your talent engaged and monogamous you must constantly work to become their "better job," the place so great they wouldn't think of leaving. As you build an exceptionally talented team, you A.R.M. your organization for battle.

## Attract

A strong, positive culture works as a self-selection tool. It naturally attracts the right people and repels bad fits. Supportive of that strong culture is a compelling purpose that you exemplify overtly. Culture is the shared values, attitudes, and beliefs of a social group. Some cultures are positive, some negative, and others fall at various points in between. Cultures can be strong or weak, depending on the depth of commitment to the values, attitudes, and beliefs of the group. A strong, positive culture is not only good for the day-to-day experience of teammates, it creates superior value for customers and serves as a talent magnet drawing the best and brightest to apply for a role in your organization.

In a 2018 report, *Executive Guidance: Culture in Action: The Role of Leaders in Making Culture Perform*, Gartner, Inc. indicates that only 31 percent of human resources managers believe their organization has the culture needed to recruit top talent. If your organization is among the other 69 percent that doesn't, you're fighting a losing battle. Top talent in business is like free agents in football. They know they are going to be paid top dollar regardless of where they go. Why would a marquee quarterback like Deshaun Watson choose the Houston Texans over all the other teams? Culture. For DW4, a winning culture and a chance to win a championship make up the right situation for him. To be clear, a great culture is less important if you want to attract mediocre talent. Not surprisingly, mediocre talent means mediocre results. To attract elite talent, build a winning culture.

People want to work for an organization that is recognized for its impact. So, at the Texans we use a powerful resource to demonstrate to prospective teammates that we are committed to providing an environment that the very best enjoy and find rewarding. Being recognized many times as one of Houston's best places to work by the *Houston Chronicle* has elevated our organization to the top ranks in the state. The application process for this designation helps us sharpen our policies and offerings for employees, thereby positioning us as an attractive organization for top talent. Our recognition as one of the city's best places to work has not only attracted new teammates, it has reinforced to our existing Texans that we intentionally work hard to meet their workplace desires.

## Retain

Keep the right people on the bus by getting the wrong people off. This is a discipline your organization must develop. You might think there is no real cost to keeping teammates who aren't a good fit, but that's just not true. Retaining stars requires you to first identify them, then to provide them with the opportunities, compensation, and resources to support their talent. Stars want to work with and for stars and they won't tolerate subpar performers taking up space, so they look to you, the leader, to make sure any issues are addressed early and decisively. The goal is to make sure that the super stars on your team never look for another job. Only you can create the environment that keeps them feeling valued, challenged, and satisfied.

## Maintain

Loyalty isn't guaranteed. Part of retaining talented staff is maintaining a workplace that builds loyalty. As you build the best team possible, use feedback from workplace surveys to ensure your environment meets their needs. Every issue expressed in the survey must be addressed, even if it cannot be resolved. It's up to you to decide what is appropriate to be done and then it's on the teammates to decide whether that decision is right for them. Everyone on the team deserves the right to be heard, but they don't have the right to get what they want. They can vote with their feet, because everyone is a free agent. Teammates can leave the organization any time they want.

Over the years, our surveys have uncovered hundreds, maybe even thousands of opportunities, big and small, for our organization to get better. What might seem small to me—"The coffee in our break room stinks!"—might be a huge deal to someone else. When I read this comment, I had to admit that I had never really thought about it. But I agreed and it was changed immediately. When we received the suggestion that our parental leave policy was not keeping up with current times, we researched, agreed, and changed it to meet the needs of our teammates. This closed-loop process informs teammates that their suggestions are heard, and it demonstrates that improvements will be made. Seeing that a request has been acted upon increases the likelihood that teammates believe their voice matters and encourages them to provide even more feedback. It is incredible to experience the appreciation, trust and loyalty generated when leadership asks, listens, and responds to workplace issues in a transparent manner. Refusing to A.R.M. your organization properly allows the potential for great teammates to seek opportunities for that better job you could have created. Once they find it elsewhere, there's no way to put the toothpaste back in the tube. You cannot recover. You've lost.

Gardeners know that providing care and feeding for plants is not enough. Weeding is a necessity. During weeding, it's best to err on the side of pulling too much than too little. Too little weeding, and the weeds take over and kill your beauties. In organizations, it's important to conduct a thorough, periodic "weeding" using a well-defined and disciplined process. It's hard to let people go, even when it's clear that it's the right thing to do. However, poor performing or misfit teammates don't fire themselves. You must regularly pull the weeds. As the leader, it's your job to make sure that both the high performers and the under performers are addressed with equal intensity.

Top talent creates the ceiling of performance for your entire organization. Everyone must be brought up to that level. After all, you're only as good as your weakest link. Stephen Schwarzman, chairman and CEO of The Blackstone Group, says in the book *King of Capital* by David Carey and John E. Morris, "Always look for tens. If you're hiring for sixes, you're going to get six results." My leadership team has an average tenure with the Texans of sixteen years. We've been in business for twenty years. It is rare that I have the chance to onboard a new teammate. When I do, our first visit covers the topic of trust, which is the glue that holds all relationships together. Between a manager and a direct report, absolute trust, both ways, must be non-negotiable. During my first conversation with a new teammate, I use my T.R.U.S.T. test to lay the foundation of our relationship. Key points I share with them are:

## Tell

Don't ever cover things up. Always tell me what I need to know. Give me the bad news immediately, and the good news whenever.

## Respect

We each have separate and important roles to play and we must always respect that.

## Understand

How you see an issue is often influenced by where you sit. That is your sphere of understanding. It's okay that you don't know a situation from every angle, but you do need to understand your role in it. Sometimes, you have to just swallow hard and embrace that there is a greater plan in play. I see things you don't. I know things you don't know. There will be some decisions I make that you do not like. Trust that there is a bigger picture and believe that I am trying to get it right all the time.

## See something, say something

I cannot be everywhere and I do not see everything. I expect you to be my eyes and ears regarding things that could be important to me. I do not expect you to report gossip or to spy. All I want is facts that can help us all do our jobs better. Don't ever let me get blindsided. Ever.

## Truth

I will always shoot straight with you and I need you to do the same. Leaving out facts and details that need to be communicated is dishonest. Don't be dishonest. I don't believe in white lies and half-truths. There is only truth and not truth. Only unvarnished honesty is acceptable.

At the Texans, we have a basic, but effective tool called the talent grid that every manager uses to evaluate each member of his or her team. Those grids are discussed by our leadership team, which is called BOLT—Business Operations Leadership Team. The goal is for us to have an objective, fact-based conversation that allows us to identify the "tails" of the bell-shaped curve—as in the outliers, both strong and weak—in all departments. Most everyone is in the middle of the bell curve and there is no real reason to have significant dialogue about these teammates. They are doing a good job. But the tails contain the stars and the duds that must be addressed quickly and decisively. This BOLT meeting launches management activity to address any teammates who reside in either of the two tails. Some industries and organizations require very specialized skills to get their work done. In a sporting environment, that matters very little compared to what we term the "non-negotiable talents." We have found through experience that three things are absolutely critical to the success of a new teammate.

First, they must have a tremendous work ethic. Legendary motion picture mogul Samuel Goldwyn once remarked, "The harder I work, the luckier I get." In any industry, there is no substitute for hard work. It cannot be taught or demanded. It shows itself in every action taken by dedicated, results-focused people who understand that progress matters more than perfection. Hard work is the silent, sometimes subtle personality trait of everyone who stretches beyond to finish the job for the team, no matter what department they're in or at what level they are on the organizational chart. That hard work should always, without fail, be recognized and rewarded by leadership.

Our second non-negotiable talent is a winning attitude—positive, optimistic, and team oriented. More often, teammates from whom we have had to separate were not technically poor performers, rather they possessed a poor attitude. Specifically, they did not have the winning attitude required to be a Texan. As with those garden weeds, keeping teammates with a poor attitude has an ill effect on the rest of the team. Weeds spread throughout the garden and often sap precious nourishment from the buds that are destined to blossom and produce fruit. Weeds often show themselves by their poor attitude. They have no place in your organization. Your responsibility is to recognize the weeds and snatch them out swiftly and often.

Lastly, we look for teammates who possess a demonstrated capacity to operate in a manner that is consistent with our values and our culture. One way we ensure this is through our maniacal focus on hiring from within. Our main pipeline for talent is our internship program, which we call the Draft Class. We search for the best and brightest recent college graduates and provide them an opportunity to spend nine months with our organization to determine if they have the work ethic, the winning attitude, and the values that align with being a Texan. If they do, we provide them with a full-time position with us, regardless of the department. One-third of our business operations employees began as interns of the Houston Texans. This provides us with an extended review of the candidate's potential, and is critical in our efforts to build and maintain the culture of our organization. One key entry point for the Draft Class is our Battle Red team of hourly workers hoping to earn a spot within the Draft Class. I have termed our approach of hiring from within, "The PEZ Dispenser approach" to talent management. Just like the PEZ candy, talent rises through the organization each time one piece is plucked from the top.

In a perfect world, all of our teammates would start as members of our Draft Class. Of course, the world is not perfect, so we do hire from the outside from time to time. In those cases, we use a combination of extensive behavioral interviews, reference checks, tests, and quantitative tools to ensure we're hiring the best fit for the position. One such tool that I am quite fond of is Caliper, but we have used Gallup's StrengthsFinder and others to help us make great hiring decisions. What I love about Caliper is they provide an analyst to review the results and make a determination if each candidate is a good fit. I call our analyst "The Sorting Hat," like the magical hat in *Harry Potter* that could tell which house was best for each kid at Hogwarts. Whatever approach you use, resist the temptation to hire too quickly. Finding great talent that fits the culture of your organization takes time. You have to invest the time to reap the rewards.

I learned an important lesson about what talent really means during my college years at Clemson University. As a kid, I had dreams of being a World Cup Soccer star, but (Spoiler alert!) just because you love something that doesn't mean it is going to love you back. I selected Clemson University because it had one of the best soccer programs in the nation and I saw it as the best opportunity for me to develop as a player. During my freshman year, I didn't play much and actually considered transferring. After the first semester, I received a letter advising me that the Dean had a list . . . and I was on it! Excited, I called my mom and told her that the Dean was keeping track of me. "Jamey, that is the Dean's List and colleges do that to recognize good students," she said, probably wondering why I hadn't figured that out by then.

Making it onto the Dean's List inspired me to focus on my studies and develop my leadership skills. I ended my time at Clemson as an honors graduate and student body president. Although I continued to play on the soccer team, I gave up my lofty ambitions of making it as a pro. For four years, I played on a soccer team that won two national championships, which taught me a lot about how championship teams are built. To win, we needed the right composition of players to get the right result. When we hoisted the 1987 National Championship Trophy, I realized we not only had the eleven best players to play the game, but we had the best eleven players to *win* the game. That's how it works in sports and that's how it works in business: the right talent, in the right roles, all doing their job and focused on getting results for the team.

In professional sports, the acquisition of talent is of utmost importance for franchises, especially in the hyper-competitive NFL. Teams of college scouts evaluate players in preparation for their annual final exam—the NFL Draft. Scouts ascertain each player's height, weight, speed, and other measurable elements. Other key elements like character, motivation, and playing scheme fit require tremendous research and judgement. Even with so much time invested in evaluating players, it is still an inherently human business. Great expectations are often followed by disappointing results. The goal isn't to get every talent decision right, but to get them more right than everyone else. The same holds true for business. Managers are typically too quick to hire and too slow to fire. They succumb to the desire to fill workforce gaps as soon as possible and simply use the "empty chair, warm body" approach to hiring. That can be costly. According to Link Humans, an employer branding firm in London, the typical cost of recruiting, hiring, and onboarding a new employee is $240,000.

Organizations that inherently hire quickly either do not have a clear vision for the right candidate or they don't maintain the discipline required to avoid settling for just okay. The "empty chair, warm body" approach to hiring is common because of pressure to fill open positions quickly. This added pressure is not good for the health of the team. Decisions regarding the talent level and fit of people for a specific role is already a risky proposition when done well, and the pressure to move fast only elevates that risk. Fortunately, I have not worked with very many teammates who operated counter to our cultural norms. But when they have, the issue was addressed immediately. The danger is not in what it eats, but what it spoils. If they won't get in line with our culture, they have to go. Most departures have not been for poor performance, but rather for things like poor values alignment.

Soon after I started with the Houston Texans, a teammate who was previously my peer was put under my direction. He was a cultural question mark during his first few months and had rubbed more than a few people the wrong way. I think Bob McNair believed I might be able to turn him around. Over dinner with my wife Melissa, I shared what had happened that day. I said, "How cool would it be if I could turn this guy into a star?" I think she admired my enthusiasm, but remained skeptical. The next day, I found out she was right. As I prepared for work, I thought through all of the relationship items I needed to share with him to get us off to the right start. The conversation began well enough and he seemed to understand and respond in a manner that was consistent with acceptance. Towards the end of the day, he mentioned wanting to release some information through our website and I asked that he hold off until I was comfortable with it. An hour later, he came back and informed me that he had indeed shared the release and justified it by saying, "I just thought it needed to get done." I responded with, "You're fired." Given the past issues that had already placed a cloud around his commitment to our corporate culture, this was really his second chance to earn my trust, considering that he did nothing to reciprocate my efforts to build our relationship as my peer. Trust is a vital part of having a high-functioning organization and it is non-negotiable with direct reports.

Imagine how much better your talent decisions would be if you employed a fraction of what an NFL teams invests in the evaluation of collegiate football players, examining a candidate's character, their motivation, and their fit before allowing them to be part of the team. Clearly define the talents of an ideal candidate in advance of your search. Perfection is not attainable, but anything you can do to improve the odds of finding the next superstar is well worth the effort. Bad hires are costly and potentially destructive. When you play to win, you lead your talent acquisition process like a scout.

# Invest in Your Leadership Team

Most of my leadership team at the Texans has been affiliated with the team since inception (roughly twenty years). They are all outstanding in their own right, but how we come together as a team has produced extraordinary results, well beyond what could have been accomplished individually.

Leading our BOLT team has been incredibly rewarding, but it has not been without its challenges. I have chosen to lead leaders, and that inherently has issues. I have purposefully stocked this group with strong personalities who offer a diversity of opinions and differing perspectives; not necessarily a recipe for harmonious interactions. But our discussions are robust and the key to making the process work lies squarely with me. There are times when we are all aligned, which is great. However, sometimes we are not, and in those instances it is on me to step up and make a call that inherently creates winners and losers. In those instances, I make the decision that I think is right and remind the team that their first allegiance is to BOLT. All decisions are ours regardless of our individual perspectives on a given issue. This is non-negotiable.

The relational health of the BOLT team is on me, too. Fortunately, they are all bright and talented. Nonetheless, I remind them of the importance of honest and authentic communication. I call out members who behave inconsistently with our charter. I help the group grow and develop. The buck stops with me regarding members who need to be removed. High-performing teams don't just happen. If you want to lead, you have to accept that it's on you to develop the environment for a winning leadership team.

To get average results, lead followers. To attain exceptional results, lead leaders. The time and effort I have invested to lead leaders has been well worth it. Years ago, we had to consider transitioning our radio broadcasting relationship, one that had served us incredibly well for a decade. In fact, we were among the league leaders in revenue, but market dynamics made it impossible for us to extend the existing deal. I had consummated the original deal in 2000, but since that time I had assumed additional responsibilities, so I assigned one of my leaders to drive the process. We talked about our options and he went away to prepare for the negotiation. What he came back with was extraordinary. His solution led to a new relationship with the same partner, which increased the value delivered to them, dramatically enhanced our brand and fan engagement, and pushed us even further ahead financially. To be the best leader you can be, you have to allow your leaders to lead.

Legendary Green Bay Packers Coach Vince Lombardi said, "If you don't do what I tell you to do, you'll be fired. And if you *only* do what I tell you to do, you'll be fired." That summarizes the dynamics when leading leaders. When you lead followers, your sole objective is to gain compliance. That's pretty easy to achieve, but it puts a low ceiling on your impact. When you lead leaders, you need them to comply with your expectations, but you also have to allow them to blaze their own path towards success. The glue that makes all of this work is trust.

As a young manager, and even after more than a decade in, I thought my job was to provide answers. After all, I was leading a team of super smart people. I thought I had to prove to them that I knew more than they did; otherwise, how could I justify my role as the leader? To say this mistaken identity of myself as the know-it-all leader kept me up at night would be an understatement. The self-imposed pressure to always have the right answer became unnerving. I felt like I was always on, always being quizzed, always being judged. But it was all in my head. No one can know everything. Admitting that to myself was a huge relief. Even now, I have to keep the know-it-all leader inside my head in check.

Every member of my staff is so close to the details of everything they do that they often come to me with questions about how to move forward with a project. So, when they come to my office and ask, "Boss, I have a problem, what should I do?" I hear a little voice in my head saying, "Don't take the bait." Humans are hardwired to provide answers when confronted with a question. Rather than give them the answer they seek, I have learned to help them reach the answer themselves. So, I ask questions that lead them to the answer. Because, after all, the question is the answer.

This might be challenging for you at first, but it gets easier with practice. Even if you immediately know the answer, your questions demonstrate to your team how to think through their problems so they can resolve issues without your help next time. Your starting questions should be focused on clarifying the challenge. Subsequent questions should lead your teammate to come up with options. And your final question should allow them to verbalize the best answer based on the information available. This series of questions could look something like this:

➢ Why is this such a problem for you?
➢ What do you think your options are?

> ➢ What are the pros and cons of each of those options?
> ➢ Which of those do you think is the best choice and why?
> ➢ What do you think you need to do from here?
> ➢ How can I help you get started?

When you apply this technique, your teammate will likely think you have solved their problem for them. That's because you asked questions. When you ask questions, you learn. When you make statements, you teach. This technique allows you and your teammates to learn together. That is what winning leaders do, help solve problems while also building the capacity of the team.

# Motivate Your Team

Successful leaders get results through others. That requires that you know how to use the power of motivation, a natural and necessary aspect of your playbook for continuous success. Most people are motivated by tools or triggers that promise a positive result for them. As quiet as it's kept, these motivating tools do not have to be large or outlandish to achieve optimal results. In fact, the more sincerity with which these tools are presented, the more motivated your team will be. Three widely used tools I have seen leaders use to motivate their teams are the three Cs: Cash, Coercion, and Commitment.

1. **Cash:** Money is important to many people, but for most it is not a key driver of motivation. It's not the best weapon in the leader's tool kit because you can pay someone to do a job, but you can't pay them to give a #%*!

2. **Coercion:** You can create an environment where everyone is scared of being fired. In this type of fear-based leadership, the magic of collaboration is non-existent (except maybe to organize a coup) because of a lack of trust. Creativity is stifled and risk taking is off the table because of the potentially negative outcomes. Everyone stays safely within

a defined box. Backstabbing runs rampant and everyone is quick to blame others. Essentially, coercion, as a motivator, is a setup for a huge fail.

3. **Commitment:** Encouraging team members to gain a deep commitment to the organization's purpose, values, and culture motivates them to get results. Commitment inspires *elective* effort. Teammates do things because they want to, they choose to. You have no shot of implementing most of the concepts in this book unless you build a committed team to work with.

At the Texans, our teammates are proud of the "whatever it takes" attitude exhibited by everyone. This attitude stems from the belief that what we are doing is big, and it matters. They care for and are committed to the McNair family, our customers, and each other. They are motivated to do their best in every situation. The reality of this was demonstrated during a very difficult time for me.

The day after Thanksgiving in 2018, I flew to Atlanta, Georgia to move my mom to Houston. Her short-term memory had deteriorated over a two-year period and we were concerned that she was developing Alzheimer's. This fear was later confirmed by the amazing neurology team at Houston Methodist Hospital. All we knew at that time was that she could no longer live on her own. My brother John and I originally thought we could find her an assisted living facility in Atlanta, but after touring several facilities months earlier, we decided she needed to come to Houston or be near John's family in Boca Raton. The choice was hers. She chose Houston. We were in the middle of football season, so I was crunched for time, but I had the move all mapped out. John, my sister Mary, my mom, and I would pack all day Friday, then my mom and I would drive to Houston on Saturday, arriving in time for the Texans to host the Tennessee Titans for Monday Night Football. Little did I know at the time that this game would become one of the most meaningful professional sports experiences of my life.

The trip started well enough. I arrived in Atlanta early Friday morning and met my brother and sister at my mom's house. We packed all day and things were going according to plan. That is, until my phone buzzed. It was our Texans public relations chief, "Jamey, I am so sorry to have to tell you this, but Bob McNair passed away this afternoon," she said. *What?* I was confused. Was she joking? If she was, I was certain that I'd light into her the moment I returned to the office. "I'm so sorry, Jamey. I know how much he meant to you," she continued. With these next words, I realized she was serious. This worst of all news was true. My heart broke. My eyes watered. A dry lump formed in my throat that prevented me from speaking. Knowing that Bob had been fighting a long and courageous battle with cancer didn't soften the blow of this news. In that moment, I was devastated.

Managing my mom's move, and now the news of Bob's death, I was broken, paralyzed with grief. My mind raced with all kinds of thoughts about what to handle next, but I was frozen. Thankfully, our amazing team at the Texans pulled together to get us moving in the right direction. They let me know exactly what they needed from me and I responded. Our public relations team crafted a statement and released it to the media. For hours that day, and well into the night, my phone blew up like it does after a win, except this time the volume of texts and emails was equivalent to every victory we ever had, all at once. It was a lot to process, but I committed to maintaining a positive focus and going forward.

The next day, my mom and I left early for the 12-hour drive to Houston. Along for the ride was her reclusive cat, Ariana, who had been her long-time companion. As much as I hated the thought of cat hair and kitty litter in every crevice of the car, there was no way we could leave Ariana behind. My mom was very clear on that.

As we pulled away from her recently sold house in her 2007 red Saturn with its balding tires, I crossed my fingers that the smooth, worn wheels would get us safely to our destination. We stopped in Jackson, Mississippi for lunch at Raising Cane's (my mom loves fried chicken) and a well-needed break from Ariana's constant meowing. As we made our way back to the freeway, I took a turn that apparently isn't legal in Mississippi. I realized my error, thanks to the glaring blue lights I saw flashing in the rear-view mirror. The state trooper calmly approached the car, then requested my license. After glancing between the photo on my license and my distressed face, he went back to his car to check things out. When he returned, he surveyed me, my mom, Ariana, and the car stuffed with half of everything my mom owned.

"Having a rough day?" he asked.

I replied, "You have no idea, officer." That's when he broke the news that added fuel to the already blazing fire: the tags on Mom's car were expired. I gulped, hard, and wanted to bang my head against the steering wheel for neglecting to check that minor detail prior to departure. With so much already on my mind, it never occurred to me that the tags had lapsed more than a year prior.

"I won't ticket you for that," the trooper said. "Just be careful." He then gave me a look that let me know he would be praying for us. At that point, we could use all the help we could get.

If you're not familiar with what Alzheimer's does to its victims, it causes them to lose their short-term memory. Something that happened just moments earlier, like a conversation, seems to be erased from memory as if it never happened. It's hard on everyone in normal circumstances. However, being in a confined space for twelve hours with someone with Alzheimer's is an especially grueling experience, especially if it is someone you love dearly. I heard the same stories and fielded the same questions from my mom every half hour. It was a tough journey. However, the long, challenging ride with my mom, whom I cherish, combined with Bob's death and the stark reminder of the fleeting nature of our existence, made me feel as if I was in an episode of *The Twilight Zone*. So much of my life was changing all at once. I had never felt so alone.

A few more hours into the drive, my phone rang. It was Bob's son Cal, who had recently been named Chairman. "Hey Jamey, we're trying to get things going here with arrangements for Dad," he said. "Do you think NRG Stadium is available to host a public service to honor him?"

Immediately, I thought that would be a great idea. The fans loved Bob as much as he had loved them. Allowing them to gather in the place that meant so much to him would be a fitting tribute. "Let me check with the County and I'll get back to you." A quick call confirmed that December 7th was open, so I called Cal back to deliver the news. When he explained what he had in mind as a tribute for his dad, I paused for what seemed like an hour. I saw the faces of my Texans teammates, who were busy finishing preparations for a nationally televised game as part of the downhill sprint of the NFL season. More importantly, I envisioned the result of their huge hearts, their can-do spirit, and their "whatever it takes" attitude. We had a lot on our plates already, and I knew that no one on our team had ever organized a funeral service in an NFL stadium. Despite all of that, I was confident my teammates would be honored to know they had been entrusted with this responsibility. In this situation, I wasn't the one who motivated my teammates. Their own commitment to the team, to the fans, and to the McNair family kept them motivated to support each other. Their motivation wasn't driven by coercion or cash. It was driven by commitment. Knowing this filled my heart with pride. "Boss, we got this," I said.

While we were full steam ahead for the season, we carved out time to prepare for a crowd of one thousand fans to say goodbye to

Bob. We had several meetings with our team and the funeral home staff. After our final planning meeting, I said to the funeral director, "This is all new to us. How are we doing?"

He replied, "Let me put it to you this way, if the Texans ever decide to get into the funeral business, we're toast!"

The Monday night game following Bob McNair's death was transformed into a celebration of the life of an incredible leader. We even had a 100-yard touchdown run by Lamar Miller against the Tennessee Titans that was punctuated by the radio call of Marc Vandermeer, the voice of the Texans, "This one's for you, Bob!" Monday, November 22, 2018 is a night I will always cherish. I could not have been prouder of how our team performed. Surprisingly, I was able to keep my emotions relatively in check over an eventful series of days leading up to the service. I managed to keep my emotions together until I stood on the field prior to beginning the Monday Night Football game and watched the incredible life tribute our team had created for Bob McNair. It was stunning.

The stadium was in total darkness as a video played on the video board. Spotlights shone down to illuminate Bob's initials, RCM, which had been painted onto the field. I totally lost it. I bent over and tears rolled down my face. I couldn't hold it back and I didn't want to. He had meant so much to me. He had changed my life. I loved him and I know he loved me. I just wanted him to walk out of the tunnel and tell me that everything was going to be okay, but that wasn't going to happen. As the lights came up, I composed myself and tried to get my mind focused on the blessing that he was to me and so many others, and of course, the important work in front of us.

The service went off without a hitch. It was beautiful. It was a fitting tribute to a man who had done so much for the Texans and for our community. I was proud of our team. Their commitment to the McNairs, our vision, and each other once again ignited their "whatever it takes" attitude. They had put forth an incredible amount of elective effort, demonstrating the kind of motivation required to be truly great.

# Exemplify the "Get-Better" Mentality

Have you ever been in a meeting when your team spent the whole time justifying why what they did was good enough; why their poor performance was not within their control; or why someone else was to blame for their failure? What a complete waste of time. When you see this, you know that your team has fallen into an acceptance mindset. This shows up when they justify why what they've done is okay. They accept that good enough is good enough, which leaves no room for improvement and keeps the entire organization at status quo. When this happens, you need to shift the mindset of your teammates. A growth focus is the essence of the get-better mentality.

To develop the get-better mentality, you and your team need a paradigm shift from acceptance to growth. With a growth mindset, you focus on learning from square one. You create a safe space where you praise your teammates and instruct them without blaming or excusing. You embrace the fact that nothing is perfect. No matter how great the outcome, there is always room for learning. This conversation allows you to look closely and comprehensively for ways to improve without allowing perfect to get in the way of better. This approach opens the door for fixing the *problems* rather than fixing the *blame*. It doesn't matter who's responsible for what went wrong. What matters is that you talk honestly about how to get better. As long as people do what they think is right, even if it doesn't work out, your entire team can learn and develop for the next time.

This get-better mentality can't only be applied when things don't go well. "Never ignore in victory what you would not ignore in defeat," are the words of ESPN basketball analyst and former NBA coach, Jeff Van Gundy. We take that to heart at the Texans. Every important initiative and outcome is evaluated to identify ways to get even better because we want to grow as an elite organization. We have adopted the military's after-action review process to ensure that we hold ourselves accountable for always getting better. It's incredibly simple and it works.

After any important activity, teams get together to discuss the initiative and try to identify how to do things better going forward. I encourage my teammates to come into the environment accepting that we're great at what we do, but we are not perfect. So, how can we get better? Having this mindset is important in honestly assessing our performance. As the saying goes, "The longest journey begins with the first step." And the first step towards excellence is an insatiable curiosity about the possibilities ahead.

# CHAPTER 3

# Build a Winning Culture

Culture is basically the shared values of a given group of people. Sounds simple, but creating a winning culture within your organization doesn't happen overnight. It isn't a magical fruit that results from planting one seed and then stepping away and hoping for the best. Building a winning culture requires intentional, consistent focus on the elements that matter most to your organization and to you as a leader. A winning culture must be envisioned, created, and cultivated in order to see the results you expect.

Developing sound habits is at the core of building a winning culture. And values are reflected in habits. Knowing this, we have intentionally created a culture founded on values and delivered through habits. For most organizations, culture is reflected in a values statement posted on a wall or on a piece of paper, which never gets operationalized. To intentionally create culture, values cannot just hang on the wall. You have to drive them into the minds and hearts of every teammate.

From my earliest experiences in organizational leadership, I learned that sound habits—what some might call systems and processes—are at the core of any company's success. Habits, when created thoughtfully, adopted widely, and executed consistently, drive productivity, innovation, learning, and growth at every level of an organization. Three habits I have adopted throughout my leadership journey are the habit of expectation, the habit of inspection, and the habit of reward. This trifecta of behavioral development has been instrumental in the success of the Houston Texans.

Setting clear expectations is the foundation for successful behavioral development. In fact, the foundational component of *12: The Elements of Great Managing* by Rodd Wagner and James K. Harter, PhD is, "I know what is expected of me at work." This is the first step towards having engaged teammates. And let's be honest, engaged employees are not commonplace. Over the past few decades, Gallup, Inc. has evaluated employee engagement in America and has found that only about one-third of employees are engaged in the work they do. That stinks because engaged employees generally enjoy their jobs more, which makes for a more harmonious work environment; they maintain a stakeholder position, which results in company-wide buy-in for growth initiatives and an all-hands-on-deck result during difficult times; and they deliver exceptional results, which positions the organization for long-term success.

The habit of inspection provides accountability for employees to deliver on the established expectations. This is not a call for micro-management. Instead, inspecting the output of employees demonstrates to them that their efforts matter to the overall result the company is hoping to achieve. And, although inspection is critical at every stage of a project, a good leader allows teammates the freedom to deviate from a plan in order to welcome creativity and innovation, as long as the result meets or exceeds expectations. As Ronald Reagan famously said, "Trust, but verify." Trust that your employees are working towards the overall goal, but verify that they have the resources, the understanding, and the focus needed to accomplish the desired outcome. Having a verification mechanism demonstrates that delivery upon behavioral expectations is important. It also allows you to fulfill the third habit, reward.

At each game we have thousands of hourly employees on hand at NRG Stadium to welcome more than seventy-one thousand fans over for lunch. We believe our expectations around "Texans-style hospitality" are very clear, but without a verification system, we would only be hoping that our staff delivers memorable experiences. That's why, since the inception of the Texans, we have used a number of tools to help us evaluate and verify the service delivery of our staff. We use secret shoppers to track the time it takes for fans to get through ticket and concessions lines, and to capture interactions with gameday employees, among other things. Many of these interactions are credibly positive and help us identify our "Spirit of Service" award winners. The rare negative is used for employee development purposes. We also have used J.D. Power for two decades to conduct "voice of the fan" research, which becomes a key input for our improvement initiatives. It also helps determine bonus/refund amounts between us and our long-time culinary partner, Aramark. These verification tools provide an objective basis for evaluating performance, and serve as the foundation of our accountability process.

Rewarding employees for delivering upon expectations creates a greater probability that those behaviors will be repeated. Even better, public rewards teach others that these behaviors are important to the whole, and that they will be recognized. This inspires others to engage in the modeled behavior. When you set clear expectations, you can identify when those expectations are delivered upon and then reward that behavior. This creates the flywheel of behavior, and these habits form the foundation of culture.

By using this concept of expect, inspect, and reward, we have built a powerful culture at the Houston Texans by employing a behavioral model called IMPACT. It is simple to understand and is something our teammates can easily execute. As an acronym, IMPACT explains our expectations for the habits our teammates are encouraged to embrace:

## Innovative

Our teammates are constantly looking for new and better ways to do things. We want them to look for opportunities to make a difference in the world and demonstrate the get-better mentality every day.

## Memorable

Everyone in the organization is encouraged to identify their talents and perform them more often so they are remembered for excellence in some capacity. Because our organization creates memories, we want teammates at every level to find a way to play a role in that.

## Passionate

Whatever your talent, do it with passion—an unabashed sincerity and authenticity that can't be faked. Passion causes people to go above and beyond the parameters of their job description to contribute their best to the company's mission, their fellow teammates, the organization, and the community.

## Accountable

Responsible, passionate teammates hold themselves accountable for higher standards of performance. In turn, they hold their teammates accountable for bringing their A-game every day.

## Courageous

Having the courage to do what's right, even when it's not popular, is a characteristic of impactful teammates. Sam Houston said it best when he defined courage as, "Do what's right and accept the consequences." Everyone in our organization is urged to have the courage to make right choices that impact themselves, the team, our fans, and ultimately the community we serve, helping us all to live by the wise words of Texans founder Bob McNair: "You can't go wrong by doing what's right."

Teammates are encouraged to do the right thing in each situation they face. When we say "right," we mean ideals such as honesty, integrity, and fairness that encompass moral behavior. If you do what's right and it doesn't work out, that's okay. We'll learn from it. Conversely, if you cheat, cut corners, lie, or otherwise engage in deceitful behaviors, there is no place for you at the Texans, regardless of the results you get. Life's too short to work with turds, and success is not sustainable without fair dealing.

## Team-first

We each have our roles to fulfill on a team, but our individual success only matters if the entire team wins. As six-time NBA champion Michael Jordan said, "Talent wins games, but teamwork and intelligence wins championships."

To drive these habits into the DNA of our teammates, we leverage the power of expect, inspect, and reward through a program called the IMPACT Awards. Every couple of months, and sometimes between those months, teammates are recognized for their IMPACT—being Innovative, Memorable, Passionate, Accountable, Courageous, and Team-first. The recognition begins when a teammate notices that one of their peers has done something exceptional and they let me know about it. That outstanding teammate will get an IMPACT Award, which comes with a $500 cash bonus. More importantly, receiving an IMPACT Award creates a platform for that employee to help everyone else understand the organization's expectations. In this way, they are living the motto of Miami Dolphins head coach, Don Shula when he said, "I know of no other way to lead than by example."

When I get a letter from a teammate saying, "Hey, I just wanted to drop you a note that so and so did this and they were awesome," it is amazing. I share these notes at our staff meetings to teach everyone what it looks like to go above and beyond for our teammates, our organization, and our fans. Sometimes, these inspiring letters come from those outside of our organization, which is equally incredible. When our community, and those we serve, are impacted by our staff, it sends a message that we are living our culture and values. When I share notes like this one, you can imagine the impact on our teammate's desire to do more good:

> *"I just wanted to drop you a note of thanks and a strong commendation of your staff that make the Houston Texans a first-class organization for all its supporters. The care and courtesy shown by Amy, Allie, and Drew was well beyond anything we could have asked for when attending the NFL Draft in Nashville last week. As a group, we have devoted our lives and made many sacrifices to fly from Scotland to*

*attend games since 2012, and we continue to do so with such excitement every year to watch this team. Win or lose, this franchise and the City of Houston have embraced us like their own. And, despite being over four thousand miles away, we've brought this team into our hearts and it means so much more than just a game now. We are all so excited to have the team play in London so we can pay back just a small part of the hospitality that the Texans community has shown us.*

*Once again, thank you for accommodating us on the incredible journey this team is on. You've made a group of lads from Scotland, Houston Texans fans for the rest of our lives."*

*~Euan de Ste Croix*

Acknowledgments like our IMPACT Awards have driven our culture into the DNA of our staff. The simple process of expect, inspect, and reward has helped encourage natural habits which have become the foundation of the powerful culture we have built. I have seen firsthand how this culture has infiltrated every aspect of our operation and has impacted every task and function at every level. To the point of lauded management consultant and author Peter Drucker, "Culture eats strategy for breakfast." Strategy certainly has its place in a winning game plan. But, for inspiring teammates to give their best at all times, creating an authentic, inclusive culture can't be beat.

A winning culture inspires teammates to show up and do their best. Your job is to find out what energizes and inspires employees to do their very best work every day. Part of this is continuously searching for ways the workplace can be improved through employee feedback. This can be a daunting task, filled with anxiety. After all, you don't want to be criticized for maintaining workplace elements that stifle creativity, productivity, and innovation. However, the feedback allows you to eliminate useless or cumbersome rules and introduce elements that energize your teammates. By simply asking the question, "How can we get better?" you provide your teammates with a voice. The result: They feel heard, and you decide which changes will be made. Everyone has a right to be heard, but they don't have the right to get what they want.

Employee surveys often yield recommendations that are both cheap and easy to satisfy. Making these changes, and communicating them to employees, can have an incredibly empowering effect. Using this simple approach, the Houston Texans have been recognized as one of our community's best places to work numerous times. This not only increases the commitment among our existing teammates, but also attracts higher-quality prospective employees to our organization.

Every other year we have a comprehensive employee survey that, among other things, asks teammates to suggest things that could make our great workplace even better. We pull out three to five of their suggestions that we can get better at, and take action on them. An important step is communicating to teammates what has been improved. This report is as simple as, "We listened to what you had to say. Here are the five things you said are really important." Following that, we keep them apprised of the progress. Later, a simple email might state, "We've already knocked out one of the improvements, and we have four more upcoming." Then, in an all-employee briefing, for example, we might share, "We've got four of these done, and we have one left." When we finally complete improvements, we communicate that and thank them for their feedback. It's really that simple.

From time to time, I drop in at different offices within our organization, just to get a feel for how things are going. One morning, while checking in at our ticket office, a teammate named Kathryn approached me and asked, "Why do we have to go upstairs to the break room to get our drinks?" Honestly, I had never thought about it, but when I did, I realized that the distance over to the break room was quite a hike just to grab a cold drink.

That day, I called a friend at Coca-Cola (one of our terrific long-time sponsors) and said, "Hey, can you deliver a Coca-Cola refrigerator to our ticket office, a really big one? I need it ASAP." Within twenty-four hours it was delivered. I knew how important this was to Kathryn, so I made sure to be there when the refrigerator arrived.

"Kathryn, here's your Coke machine," I said. Her eyes widened and a bright smile crossed her face.

"Holy cow!" she said.

That one simple idea was easy to implement and it cost the organization very little. With that small act, the entire ticket office staff, among others, realized that sharing a good idea can change things pretty quickly. The best part is the communication that happens. Teammates feel heard, respected, and appreciated. If something is important and we can do it, we will do it.

Our employees have often mentioned in surveys that there is never time to take a break. In today's hyper-connected world—with smart phones, tablets, Wi-Fi, Bluetooth, and other technological advances that encourage 24/7 connectivity—we have created an environment in which we are always reachable. Consequently, it feels like there is no escaping the workplace, even when you're at home or on vacation. As our leadership team reviewed issues from our employee survey, a suggestion was made that we consider closing our office the entire week of Independence Day. Coaches and players are on their summer break. Most of our customers and clients are on vacation as well. And, preparation for the upcoming football season doesn't become crazy-busy until mid-July. Much of the communication within the organization is internal. With our offices empty, and our external constituents away, we concluded that we might have a good shot of providing everyone with the opportunity to be disconnected.

As we explored the idea, it became clear that this was the ideal way to provide a much-needed break for everyone. But the only way this could work was with the full commitment of every department. Everyone had to stand down from communicating with each other unless it was absolutely necessary. Everything except an emergency must wait. Once everyone agreed, we moved forward, deciding that this would be a one-time experiment. We tested it, and it worked like a charm. Selfishly, I might have been the most delighted with the outcome. It turned out to be an amazing way to allow our team to unplug and return refreshed and ready to be awesome. We've done this continuously for over a decade with tremendous results and appreciation by all our teammates.

Helping employees be their best and perform at the top of their game is important for me. For some teammates, that means having the ability to work from home. I must admit, given our collaborative environment, I never believed working from home was for us. There is a certain and necessary dynamic that happens when everyone involved in a project assembles in the same space to get the work done. That's pretty old-school, but it's always worked for me. My perspective changed as a result of the coronavirus pandemic that swept the globe in 2020, causing a huge chunk of the American economy to shut down immediately, and forcing organizations to enact a plan C they never thought would be necessary. With just seventy-two hours notice from the governor of Texas, our organization, which would never have considered a company-wide work-from-home ordinance, was transformed into performing one hundred percent virtually. Talk about an adjustment!

Although there was a bit of a learning curve, after a few weeks, almost the entire organization was operating at near full strength. Video conferencing replaced in-person meetings for everything from department meetings and recaps to sales and service calls with clients. We even had the first-ever virtual NFL Draft and virtual off-season program with our players. It wasn't perfect, but it proved to me that working virtually can and will be part of our mix going forward. In fact, some positions shifted to work exclusively from home and now only come to the office periodically for certain meetings and company gatherings. As the saying goes, "Necessity is the mother of invention."

Every leader relies on a system, process, or approach to execute projects effectively. Leave it to your team to figure out how to get from point A to point B, and they'll do it. But you need a system for knowing that the work is done to the expected outcome. The golf pro at Galveston Country Club, Donnie St. Germain, says the key to golf is a repeatable swing. It is the same with business execution. You need to have tools and a process that facilitates the achievement of consistent results. My informal approach to manage through the execution of a strategy—most of which I have begged, borrowed and stolen from work experiences, school, reading, and conversations with other leaders—will be a helpful start.

# Ready, Set, Pivot

Darwinism, or the law of natural selection, is often a misunderstood concept. Maybe it's because it is often termed "survival of the fittest." In fact, Darwin's principle was not about the biggest or the fastest when he pronounced the survival of the fittest. Throughout time, the species that have survived have been those that have been able to adapt. In our ever-changing world, the ability to adapt has become more essential than ever. Today's business environment has given a new name to adaptability. We call it the pivot. Essentially, pivoting requires a plan and the agility to make changes when needed. As a leader, pivoting isn't always your first option, but in some instances it's your best.

At the Houston Texans, one hallmark we are committed to is having one of the best tailgating environments in the NFL. Tailgating is a key differentiator for the spectator experience at a football game. From a business perspective, tailgating offers us an incredible competitive advantage over other sports and entertainment offerings. From our first game in 2002, the quality of our tailgating experience has been far and away the most highly rated aspect of our game experience. Each week during the season, we welcome roughly thirty thousand fans into our parking lots more than three hours prior to kickoff for every home game.

Our environment quickly shifted in 2010 when an empty lot across the highway from our stadium, what was then Reliant Park, was leased to a local ticket broker. He went on local television to encourage fans without game tickets to park in his lot and then walk over to Reliant Park for our highly valued tailgating experience. The numbers of non-ticketed fans entering our parking gates by foot on game day were low to begin with. But, as we entered the regular season, we saw five thousand, then ten thousand fans fill the lots for the sole purpose of taking part in our prized pre-game tailgating experience, which had been reserved for ticketed fans. When we played the Dallas Cowboys, twenty thousand people entered our parking gates without tickets or intention to attend the game. The parking lot was a mad house. After the game, many fights broke out, and as I tried to leave Reliant Park it was clear to me that we had a problem.

Over the next few days, our team considered a number of ways to address this existential threat to tailgating. Most of the ideas were rejected. One of our operating partners suggested sheepishly, "You're not going to like this, but we could make the entire park a ticketed campus on game day." That was it. That was the adaptation required for tailgating to survive. We got busy hiring and training staff, acquiring the necessary infrastructure and materials, and then we announced the plan to the community. Sure, there were naysayers and there was some criticism, but our focus was making sure our season ticket members enjoyed the experience. We knew this was the best way to protect the gameday ritual they loved so much.

Two weeks after we played the Cowboys we played the New York Giants. All fans approaching Reliant Park by car or on foot were required to have a game ticket to enter. Because of the intense public interest in this issue, we scheduled a press availability following the game. Media members combed the parking lots, and our fans enthusiastically shared that they were thrilled with our new approach. In fact, the feedback was so positive that the media did not even attend the post-game availability. We had quickly adapted to address the changing environment. We eliminated a threat—non-ticket holders interrupting a peaceful tailgating experience—satisfied our paying customers, and avoided a potential media nightmare, all because our team pivoted swiftly to adapt in the face of change. To this day, tailgating remains a cherished Houston Texans tradition.

# Invest in R&D

Working for a company like Procter & Gamble was a great learning experience for me back in my twenties. It was an honor to be a manager at a well-recognized, global consumer products company. I was dead set on absorbing everything I could about how a brand is managed and how I could contribute my smarts to making it even better.

During my first meeting with one of our category managers, all of the new hires were around the table at lunch. Every word he said sunk into each of us like pearls of wisdom. He had been at the company long enough to know how things worked, and I wanted to know what he knew. "You're the best and brightest," he said to the group. "Let me ask you a question. In school, if you copy someone else's work, what happens to you?" We looked around, each knowing the obvious answer, but wondering if this was a trick question.

Finally, someone answered, "You get expelled."

"You're right!" he said. "But do you know what happens here at Procter & Gamble when you copy?" Silence filled the dining table. He looked left to right, then smiled a sly grin. "You get promoted! We call it 'search and reapply.'"

P&G had a huge library with the best marketing ideas of all time within the company. Whenever a successful initiative was completed, someone would write it up and it would go into the library. Anyone working on a project could go to the library and review all the things that were similar to their current project. If they found one that worked, "search and reapply" was the ticket to the fast track. This was a genius way of growing a new initiative by repeating a process that worked in the past, saving a boatload of time and effort by avoiding reinventing the wheel. Essentially, P&G's approach fit right into artist Pablo Picasso's mindset. He famously said, "Good artists borrow, great artists steal."

When I moved into professional sports, I took P&G's concept of search and reapply with me. However, I wanted to name it something that was more interesting, descriptive, and memorable. Search and reapply is really a cheap and easy form of R&D, "rip off & do better." We go to stadiums—football, baseball, basketball, hockey, soccer—and observe the experiences organizations create to determine what works and how we can replicate those ideas in our environment. Our business is simple at the Texans: Build our brand, engage our fans, and drive revenue. We are constantly looking for successful concepts that fit into one of these three buckets. When we find one, we adapt it and reapply it. Picasso! More times than not, it works even better in our environment. Sure, we give up the pride of authorship, but with a focus on playing to win, I prefer to start with a proven winning concept. That's the magic of search and reapply.

Beneficial search and reapply concepts don't even have to come from within your industry. A number of years ago, we were frustrated about the quality of our model for Club-level in-seat wait service at NRG Stadium. We conducted a learning journey to McDonald's to review their drive-thru operation to see what we could R&D. We found a number of technological, process, and training gaps in our system that became the foundation of a revamped operation for us the next season. Making a change within an organization, no matter the size, can be as simple as that.

Acknowledge the problem, decide to fix it, brainstorm ideas, conduct a bit of search and reapply, take action, and assess.

If you want to recreate the wheel, have at it. But, as you look to deploy your get-better mentality, know that there are great ideas everywhere. With subtle adaptations, you can quickly search and reapply to keep your organization poised to play to win.

# See Something, Say Something

Appreciation is a fundamental human need in all aspects of life, including in the workplace. In fact, the Gallup organization's Q12 Engagement Survey suggests that all employees need praise at least once every seven days to maintain high workplace satisfaction. All teammates have an intense desire to be appreciated for what they do. Contrary to the belief of many, compliments do not lead to a decrease in effort, but rather an increase in attention to the things that matter most. What gets rewarded gets done. The best way to extinguish a behavior is to ignore it. Unknowingly, managers who fail to recognize their teammates regularly and authentically, unconsciously push those positive behaviors towards extinction.

The power of appreciation is so significant to my leadership style that I have created several opportunities within our organization to make it a habit. We call it a culture of appreciation. To operationalize it, each employee is given a wristband with two phrases: Culture of Appreciation—See Something, Say Something. If you see someone do something that you appreciate, you are to say so. This could be as simple as saying, "Great job," "Thank you," or "I like what you did." If you miss the opportunity, you have to take the wristband from one arm and place it on the other. This is a subtle reminder that simple, positive affirmations that go unsaid are lost opportunities to teach, inspire, and energize others.

Years ago, I had the opportunity to lead a seasoned executive, who I will call Mark. He came under my direction relatively late in his career and had a hard-wired way of doing things. Although Mark was talented in his area of expertise, he was hard on his teammates. Let's say he was a management nightmare. He would rarely give compliments, more likely criticism and reprimands. He would never recognize success until a job was fully completed and he would never celebrate anything other than what he considered perfection. As a result, Mark's department was a revolving door. However, I believed he had the ability to change his perspective and approach as a manager and leader. Through intensive coaching, I helped Mark realize his own worth. Our conversations revealed that Mark's compromised self-esteem manifested in his treatment of others. Rather than focus on why and how he should improve his self-image, I focused on affirming his strong points, assuring him that he was bringing some valuable gifts to the workplace and to his interactions with the team.

"Mark, you have vast experience in this field," I told him. "You understand things far beyond the current capacity of your staff. It's not fair to expect your team to measure up to your personal standard." He looked at me puzzled, and then he began to accept my premise. "Actually, your knowledge level is far beyond what your team can comprehend, so go slow with them. Be patient. Be the example for them to aspire to." In no time, Mark started to see himself for what he was, the leader of the department. He then became a coach and a mentor to his team, rather than a bully. He accepted that they needed time and space to develop the skills to match his ability, thereby achieving exceptional goals to support the entire organization.

Given that praise encourages a repeat of positive behaviors, why are so many leaders terrible at giving it? Some think a "thank you" or a bonus for a job well done leads to laziness. Others are reluctant to compliment incomplete or proximate success. Still others are insecure and feel there's not enough praise to go around. Whatever the reason, don't ignore the positive results of encouragement. One result of praise is that it makes people feel good about their work and their contribution to the team. The best leaders know that positive feedback and encouragement are important tools to communicate expectations and drive commitment. Be the leader who uses authentic praise to hardwire positive behaviors into your teammates.

# CHAPTER 4

# Create Raving Fans

Whether you realize it or not, you probably use a number of Procter & Gamble products each day. Just take a look at the packaging for your favorite soap, detergent, dog food, toothpaste, diapers, or shavers and you'll find the P&G logo. With products recognized globally, P&G created the concept of a brand and brand management. During my tenure there, I learned of a critical success factor for any business: trial and loyalty. Using advertising, promotions, and other elements of the marketing mix, Procter & Gamble encourages consumers to try their products. But their influence on the buying decisions of households doesn't stop there. The product has to perform for the consumer so they are compelled to buy it again and again, and become a loyal customer, essentially, a raving fan.

I took those learnings with me from my time at P&G to launch the Columbus Crew. We focused squarely on the trial of our product. We were a new team, in a new league, and in a market playing host to a major league sport for the first time. We had to convince the public that we were there for them. We must have done something right because our first season was a breakthrough success. We had great attendance, earned a playoff berth, and created a fan-centric experience that generated strong loyalty. By my last season—five years later—we had the largest season ticket base in the league.

As president of the Texans, the situation was different, as we returned the NFL to Houston in 2002. This town already knew what it was like to have a winning team to call their own. But it had been four years since the Houston Oilers had departed. I was pretty confident that fans would try us, but would they come back and demonstrate loyalty behaviors? I figured that would take some doing, given the unceremonious departure of the Oilers, plus the fact that expansion teams in the modern NFL face difficulty winning early in their history. Remember the Cleveland Browns of the late 90s and 2000s? If we were to chart a course to become the most respected and most valuable sports franchise on the planet, we would have to deliver an experience, a service level, and a customer relationship that would transcend team performance. We not only wanted to attract fans, we wanted to create *raving* fans.

We started with conducting extensive research with football fans, past Oilers customers, and others to understand the experience they were looking for from us. What would make them fall in love with the Houston Texans? Our positioning statement served as a guiding light for the loyalty-building efforts we developed early in the launch of the team:

> *The Houston Texans NFL team is built for our fans. Our brand of football is authentically Texan and reflects a modern spirit for pride, strength, courage, tradition, and independence. We deliver a world-class experience through constant innovation, active involvement in the community, and a personal relationship with our fans.*

This is a bold proclamation. Our goal from day one has been to exist for our fans. Every fan, every time. To this day, our efforts begin and end with them. Our translation of loyalty building from day one had to be clear, relatable, and inspiring. So, we developed the concept of creating raving fans. This imperative influences the daily activities of the Houston Texans to this day. Loyal customers don't happen by accident, they are attracted through intentional, authentic action. The imperative for everyone on our staff is to constantly be on the lookout for opportunities to make a difference for our customers. Raving fans are not merely lovers of the game of football, they are evangelists for our entire organization. In essence, everyone's charge is to do something so exceptional that our customers feel compelled to tell someone else about it. That is the measure of a raving fan.

NRG Stadium has a seating capacity of over seventy-two thousand. Assigning seats for season ticket holders was no small feat for our first season. Our ticketing and events chief briefed me on our options. "We could have the ticketing partner place everyone in their seats," he said. I asked how long that would take. "About a minute," he replied nonchalantly. I was sure one minute would actually be more like a week, but I didn't press him. Option number two, he explained, would be to invite every season ticket member over to a sales center so they could select their own seats. It would be expensive and it would take six months. The answer was clear. Allowing fans the privilege of selecting their own seats would be a win for them and a win for us. This engagement would give fans even more of a buy-in with the team, allowing them to choose the view of the field they valued most, and it would give our staff the chance to shine as customer service representatives.

Building loyalty sometimes means you look for ways to put others in control. Sure, this can put you into a vulnerable situation, but if that is a concern, it really isn't a true partnership or a loyal relationship to begin with. Loyal relationships that create raving fans are the foundation of a strong business. In the end, the relationship drives value. It doesn't just happen. It requires intentional effort, and the relationship must be protected at all costs. Our aim was to create raving fans, and we meant it. The result? With sixty-seven thousand season ticket members, we have sold out every game we have ever played. The icing on the cake is that we have a wait list of thirty-two thousand. All of this in a market that lost an NFL team because of a history of inconsistent local support.

A Texans fan named Andrew wrote a letter to us about his experience becoming a season ticket holder. It is a great illustration of the impact of a sustained focus on creating raving fans over a long period of time:

*On Monday, Charlie Hartland called my home for my father Ruben to inform him that he had finally reached the top of the [season ticket] waitlist after about eight years of waiting. My mother, Geraldine, answered the phone and was so excited when Charlie broke the news that we now had the opportunity to become a part of the Houston Texans family. She started screaming and yelling for me to come to the phone to listen.*

*As we started talking, Charlie asked what prompted us to sign up on the waitlist all those years ago. We told Charlie that my father and I had been die-hard fans of the Texans for years. Every year, when the waitlist re-registration email was sent to us, Dad would come to me and update me on our current spot on the waitlist. It became a tradition for us. We would see how much closer we would get each year and guess when our time would finally come.*

*My father unfortunately passed away in April, only two months before we finally reached the top of the list. Dad had left me some money in his will that was to be used to purchase season tickets when we got the chance. I am so very grateful for Charlie's call this year and extremely excited to be a Houston Texans season ticket member this coming year. Cheering on the Texans at NRG Stadium will always make me think of my dad and the moments together as we waited our turn. Thank you Houston Texans.*

*Sincerely,*

*Andrew*

If I had a nickel for every time someone inside or outside of the sports industry said, "Win, and they'll come. Lose, and they won't come," I would be a very rich man. Our results at the Texans stand in stark contrast to that belief. As of the end of the 2019 season, our combined record was 131 - 157, a winning rate of 45 percent. However, if you consider a sold-out season as a *business* victory, our organization has gone 19 - 0. Our fans expect a highly differentiated experience that is akin to a mini-vacation from reality. We understand very clearly what our fans are looking for on game day and we are constantly working to build our experience to those specifications. We work hard to make them feel like family. Everyone wants to be part of something bigger than themselves, and we offer that.

We can even turn *visiting* fans into raving fans as evidenced by this fan note:

*My daughter and I drove in from Dallas on Sunday to attend the game. I have been to other professional venues, but without a doubt, the Houston Texans fans are the most polite, most fun, and most enthusiastic fans I have ever seen. It was a pleasure to spend time among them in the stadium. No one was rude to my daughter (who was wearing an "enemy jersey"). The excitement of the Houston fans was contagious. Even when the team was trailing before the big comeback, the atmosphere in the stands and on the concourse was never mean or bitter or sad. You have turned me into a Houston Texans fan. Go Texans! Thank you for your hospitality.*

There's something to be said for turning first-time visitors into raving fans. Our culture really is contagious, and we exude it in every aspect of our team. So, it was no surprise that after a few years, create raving fans started to become part of our organizational DNA, reaching into all of our internal departments. World-class internal customer service is a great foundation for high levels of collaboration and teamwork. When teammates understand that they are serving others on the team—whether in the same or different departments—the levels of commitment, service, and work quality rise substantially. Our internally focused service departments often receive high praise from their teammates for being raving fan role models. These are passionate problem solvers who go above and beyond to support and help others. Here is one of the many IMPACT Award nominations I have received through the years.

*"'IT Customer Service'" might seem like an oxymoron, but not for Bobby Rawlinson. Bobby has been the*

*consummate team player from day one, and he constantly models the IMPACT habits. He is always looking to improve the IT experience here at the Houston Texans and he has definitely elevated the service level and the tangible benefits we all receive from the technology provided to us. Each time I've interacted with Bobby, his complete attention to me has been amazing and much appreciated. Also, his willingness to explain in detail his assessment of the issue and the solution has given me comfort that my problem has been addressed with the utmost professionalism. If he was a doctor, his bedside manner would be off the charts and his patient outcomes would be similarly impressive. Bobby's positive attitude is infectious and he makes everyone around him better, inside and outside of IT."*

When I give talks about the Texans way of doing things, the conversation eventually turns to external and internal customer service, which is not surprising, given our reputation. I'll ask the audience, "How many of you would like to have a copy of the Houston Texans' customer service handbook?" Everybody's hand goes up. "Here's some good news," I tell them. "It's environmentally friendly, and it doesn't cost anything. It's only three words—create raving fans.

## Satisfaction Vs. Loyalty

My wife Melissa and I have been married for over twenty years. Ask me if we have a satisfied marriage and I would say, "No." Satisfaction gets you someone who will stay with you, unless a better option becomes available. Not a stable place to be in the most important relationship in life. I would say we have a loyal relationship. Loyalty gets you so much more than mere satisfaction. First, you stay together longer because of the deep connection that exists. You appreciate each other so much that you are compelled to tell your friends. And you are constantly looking for new things to do together. I'll take loyalty all day long over mere satisfaction.

The same is true in business. The evidence is revealed in the balance sheet of a loyalty-focused company as a line item called "goodwill." It is the value that balances a company's assets versus their liabilities plus equity. Often, a loyalty leader's goodwill is filled with loyalty value. How much is it worth? In an article in the January-February 2020 issue of *Harvard Business Review* titled "Are You Undervaluing Your Customers?" noted loyalty expert Rob Markey, Partner with Bain & Company, shares that loyalty leaders grow revenues two and a half times faster than their industry peers and deliver a two to five times greater shareholder return over the next ten years. How does that happen? Simple: loyalty economics.

Loyalty provides incredible advantages to an organization, but these benefits are realized only if leaders lift their sights from creating mere customer satisfaction to building sustained advocacy. When you build a loyal relationship with a customer, you move beyond a transaction or an exchange of value. Think about your favorite restaurant, clothing store, automobile brand, or any other product or service that is important to you, where you have been consistently provided an exceptional experience. Because of the loyal relationship that has been developed between you and that company, the company will likely have earned the following benefits which are the foundation of loyalty economics:

**Retention:** Loyal customers tend to stay with you longer because you fulfill a need in an exceptional way. They also are typically much less expensive to service, and the cost to acquire a retained customer is absolutely zero.

**Referrals:** I love to introduce people to all types of products and services that have earned my loyalty. I see it as a great service to my friends because I am confident they will have the same high-quality experience I've had. Positive word of mouth is much more persuasive at generating trial than any advertising or promotion, and it doesn't cost a cent.

**Related sales:** Your loyal customer base creates a trust that can become an entirely new platform for growth. Loyal customers know that you are committed to them. so they naturally give you an opportunity to serve their related needs. Again, your cost of acquisition is nothing.

A few years back, I had the pleasure of attending a talk by John Paul DeJoria at my friend Javier Loya's house. It was an over-the-top production with some outstanding content. DeJoria came from nothing and built a business—Paul Mitchell hair care products—out of the back of his car. He then catapulted Patrón tequila into a breakthrough success through his philosophy of loyalty centered on creating repeat customers. "I never wanted to be in the sales business," he said. "I wanted to be in the reorder business."

No one reorders a crappy product. Customers don't return to your storefront if the service is bad. Fans don't return to the stadium if they aren't treated well, and they don't support a team year after year if the experience doesn't fulfill something deep within. Inspiring customer loyalty to the point that they reorder, return, and tell a friend takes far less effort and expense than you might think. It takes a sincere desire to serve and a commitment to exceed expectations. Loyalty building creates raving fans, and a robust base of raving fans is a foundational part of continuous business success.

# Be Extra-Ordinary

In the process of achieving victory, you and your team must go beyond the expected; otherwise, there is no growth. Essentially, you have to be extra-ordinary. The Cajuns have an awesome word for it—lagniappe (lahn-yap), a little bit extra. Lagniappe can be exhibited and delivered in different ways depending on the situation. Create the environment for your teammates to step up, be creative, and take action to improve any circumstance for the customer, any customer, including internal teammates. This demonstrates an authentic and consistent focus on growth for the betterment of the organization.

Nothing and no one is perfect. Sometimes things go wrong, customers don't get what they want, someone has a bad day, or circumstances out of your control turn a normal interaction into a nightmare. When this happens, you must initiate a recovery because there is no room for ignorance in your leadership portfolio. You can't afford to ignore a problem and hope it goes away. You have to take action. According to *Inc. Magazine*, it takes forty positive customer experiences to overcome the damage of just one negative review. Forty to one! Imagine the time and dollar investment that can result from one negative review or experience. With the right attitude, and a focus on being extra-ordinary, you can turn that negative experience into a positive result for the customer and a growth opportunity for your organization.

View service recovery as a challenge that leads to change that enables growth. It is critical to have an attitude that demonstrates your commitment to extra-ordinary service. A complaint is a gift, a cry for help, an opportunity to show what you and your organization are made of. So, it is critical to fix problems and repair customer relationships when things don't go as planned. Here is a simple way to do it.

1. **Listen and let them run out of gas**, like a marlin on the line. Until they do that, they're not going to be open to what you want to propose.
2. **Think creatively**. Wow any unsatisfied customer. What can you do that would make someone say, "Wow, I can't believe you're willing to do that for me!" It doesn't have to be expensive. You have to do something that rings a bell and exemplifies thoughtfulness.
3. **Execute.** You can't just make a promise, you have to take action and make sure it happens. You have to execute it. Deliver above the expected. The goal is to be extra-ordinary.

The first step is to fix the *customer*, then you can fix the *problem*. Address their emotions regarding the situation. Identify what is important to them, and look for a window to get them back on track. Customers who have expressed a complaint provide the most fertile opportunities to create a raving fan, an ambassador, a champion who will sing your praises and enhance your reputation in powerful ways.

Disney is my hero brand. They're the gold standard for customer service, which is why my family and I love to visit Walt Disney World. Eight years ago, Melissa, Chris, Caroline and I took a trip to Orlando and stayed at Disney's Contemporary Resort. As a kid, I had friends who stayed at the Contemporary while on vacation. From that time, I dreamed of visiting that resort, but a trip like that was not within our family budget. So, when I was able to go there with my family, I was totally jacked. At check-in, we received special room keys for each guest with their name printed on the key. We all thought that was super cool, but when we got settled into the room, I noticed they had misspelled my son's name on his key. Absolutely certain they would quickly replace the key with a corrected one, I headed down to the front desk and asked the attendant if she could have the key reprinted. "I'm so sorry, but those are done by a third party," she said. "We can't have them reprinted." I was stunned and beyond disappointed at her reply.

"No, no, you don't understand," I said. "This is my son, he's eight, this is really important to him. He'll be devastated if his sister Caroline's key is correct and his isn't." The desk attendant apologized and reiterated that there was nothing she could do. I replied, "Man, you don't know how disappointed I am right now. You are the gold standard for customer service. You're supposed to do whatever it takes to make me happy."

Whether because of her embarrassment, her compassion for me and my family, or her fear that I might report the faux pas to a manager and get her fired, she quickly snapped out of her fog of "There's nothing I can do," and suddenly said, "Oh yeah, that's right, we're Disney!" Within a few hours, a new key was delivered to our room with the correct spelling of my son's name. Crisis averted. Everyone was happy. For Disney, the concept of creating raving fans is central to their brand, but doing it with every fan every time is a difficult task.

To be a true loyalty leader, everyone on the team must always be on high alert for opportunities to fix small problems before they become big ones, and to be extra-ordinary by adding a little lagniappe. Being extra-ordinary doesn't just happen. It takes intentional, inspired effort. My deep loyalty to Disney caused me to step up and fight to get them to do the right thing. Imagine how disappointed I would have been if my hero brand had let me down. That's what loyalty does. Your customers will fight to help you get it right because they desperately want to maintain their valuable connection to you.

# Brand Building = Loyalty Building

Raving fans don't just grow out of nowhere, they have to be attracted to your organization. They have to know your brand. And that brand begins on the inside with your values, your culture, and your teammates. That is inside-out branding. People don't typically put two and two together to realize that brand and loyalty are really synonymous concepts. Brand building = loyalty building.

Contrary to common thinking, a brand is not a logo, an identity, or even the product itself. A brand is an individual's connection to a product, service, or company. It is a promise to perform and basically consists of the sum total of all impressions shaped by every interaction. It is your gut feeling about a product, service, or company. When I mention Disney, what thoughts or feelings do you immediately have? How about Apple? Facebook? Nike? If you are aware of these brands (and who isn't?), you have an automatic, gut-level reaction to each of them that are your perceptions based on your experiences. So, how do great brands create raving fans?

A number of years ago, I attended a speaking engagement with Howard Schultz, former chairman and chief executive of Starbucks. He said something that solidified my thinking on brands and how they are created: "Brands are built from the inside out." Logos, colors, typefaces, and other elements of an identity are often what is mistaken for the brand, but these are just symbols that represent the brand. Ralph Waldo Emerson summed up brand building well when he said, "What you do speaks so loudly I cannot hear what you are saying." Starbucks is a great example of the power of brand building (and how it is done), and thereby, loyalty building. Growing from a single coffee shop in 1972, by 2020 Starbucks touted roughly thirty-one thousand stores around the world, over one hundred-thirty thousand employees, and a market cap north of $100 billion. Starbucks took an important step to build its brand using its "5 Ways of Being" initiative that all employees were expected to follow.

That set the groundwork for Starbucks' amazing culture. The 5 Ways of Being was an essential foundation of Starbucks' efforts to brand build from the inside out.

1. Be Welcoming
2. Be Genuine
3. Be Considerate
4. Be Knowledgeable
5. Be Involved

To drive this expectation into the DNA of every employee, the Starbucks leadership inspected for it and rewarded it. These are the habits that have allowed Starbucks to "out-behave" its competition and "habit" its way into a world-class brand that, according to the *Global 500 2019* report from Brand Finance, was worth $39.8 billion in brand value alone!! Importantly, these five expectations were designed to create customer loyalty, which has translated into an imminently valuable brand that influences every interaction with consumer.

The key point here is, whether yours is a professional sports team trying to create raving fans and earn customer loyalty or a global packaged goods company trying to drive consumer demand, success comes down to trial and loyalty. When I talk about the Houston Texans "machine" which has delivered exceptional results over two decades, the key components of that machine are our people and our loyal customer relationships. That is what creates value. Nearly every one of our major sponsors and broadcast partners has been with us for our entire existence, through numerous renewals, some dismal seasons, and the ever-changing dynamics of the economy. That is tremendous loyalty and that loyalty is valuable. As management guru, Peter Drucker observed, "Because its purpose is to create a customer, the business enterprise has two—and only two—basic functions: marketing and innovation. Marketing and innovation produce results; all the rest are 'costs.'"

# GALLERY

Rootes delivers the Chairman's address to over 1,000 business leaders to lay out the economic development, public policy, and international relations game plan of the Greater Houston Partnership for the year.

Rootes shares his perspectives on leadership with students at Saint Thomas High School in Houston. His son, Christopher, is a 2020 graduate of STHS.

Texans legend, Andre Johnson and Grammy Award Winner, Big Boi from OutKast, join Rootes for Houston Texans pre-game festivities at NRG Stadium.

Cal McNair (Texans Chairman & CEO), Jack Easterby (Texans EVP, Football Operations) and Rootes celebrate another AFC South Championship post-game in the locker room.

Rootes is joined by soccer icon, Ashley Cole, for a Texans game at NRG Stadium.

Rootes and rapper, Flo Rida, enjoy a Houston Texans game at NRG Stadium.

Rootes poses with Tyler Hubbard and Brian Kelley, better known as Florida Georgia Line, at the Super Bowl. As a huge country music fan, Rootes' daughter, Caroline, was particularly impressed with this one.

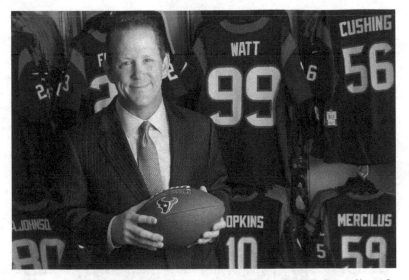

Rootes poses in the Houston Texans Team Shop at NRG stadium for a business feature in the Houston Chronicle.

Rootes and his father, Jack, attend NFL Honors at the Super Bowl.

Rootes poses at a Super Bowl brunch with actor, Ryan Reynolds. Rootes sent his wife, Melissa, a text with the question, "Which of these two was recently named the *Sexiest Man Alive*?" To which Melissa replied, "The one in the glasses." Well played!

Rootes receives the Steinberg DeNicola Humanitarian Award from sports agency icon, Leigh Steinberg, and star Alabama wide-receiver, Jerry Jeudy.

Rootes addresses the media during his annual, "What's New at NRG Stadium" press conference. The Texans work hard to ensure that the Texans Experience at NRG gets better every year for the fans and the community.

Rootes is joined by Clay Walker and the Gatlin Brothers at the NFL Owner's Party before Super Bowl LI in Houston.

Rootes poses with rapper, Lil Jon, before a home playoff game at NRG stadium. Lil Jon's song "Turn Down For What" has become a staple of the in-game experience as the team celebrates the heroics of future Hall of Famer, J.J. Watt.

Rootes celebrates with Houston rapper, Travis Scott, during a Texans victory at NRG stadium.

Rootes enjoys a Texans home game with professional Mixed Martial Artist Champion, Derrick Lewis.

Rootes and his wife, Melissa, join Texans Founder, Bob McNair and his wife, Janice, for Super Bowl festivities in Houston.

Fans show their heartfelt appreciation for Texans Founder, Bob McNair. This was taken at the first game after Mr. McNair's passing.

Rootes poses for a publication at NRG Stadium.

Rootes is joined by the family of "Joe Texan," one of the team's most ardent supporters since inception, following his recent passing. Rootes, Joe's family, and many friends gathered at his normal tailgate spot to remember his life and to reflect on the impact that Joe Texan had on all of us.

Rootes connects with game day entertainers Blanco Brown and Parmalee.

Rootes enjoys the Texans Experience with rapper, T-Pain.

Rootes and his family are joined by iconic rapper, Vanilla Ice. Ice, Ice, Baby!

Rootes hosts a true American hero, Chuck Yeager, for a Texans game at NRG Stadium. The team honored General Yeager in-game as part of their broad platform to show support for our men and women in uniform who protect our freedom.

# CHAPTER 5

# A Winning Playbook for Handling Adversity and Success

At 7:30 a.m. on Wednesday, March 11, 2020, I participated in one of the first ever virtual meetings of the Greater Houston Partnership Executive Committee. The Partnership is Houston's leading business organization, with a board that consists of one hundred, twenty CEOs from Houston's leading companies and organizations. I served as board chair several years ago, and I have a passion for the work of the Partnership.

At this virtual meeting, the normal public policy and economic development agenda was hijacked by a discussion regarding the potentially devastating impact of a new and highly contagious virus. It was hypothesized that this virus, the novel coronavirus, could overrun the capacity of our local health system. I was skeptical. I thought, "We have the largest medical center in the world. Only something of biblical proportions could exhaust our medical capacity." As I learned, COVID-19 was pounding Europe, especially Italy, but we had yet to have a documented case in Houston. That was about to change.

With hundreds of large events scheduled throughout the city, the discussion turned to whether the Houston Livestock Show and Rodeo—the largest event of its type in the world and an incredibly important event for our region—would be one of the first to shut down. The Rodeo, our partner at NRG Stadium, has been an annual ritual since 1932. The thought of shutting it down was surreal. By midday, the city had closed the Rodeo because one person in the Greater Houston area had tested positive for COVID-19, had not travelled internationally, but had recently visited the Rodeo's World Championship Bar-B-Que Contest. Community spread had begun. It was now clear to me that this was serious and it was time for us to act. Little did I know this was the tip of the iceberg.

As the gravity of the situation started to sink in, my primary concern was the safety of our staff. We had to find a way for all our teammates to work from home and we had about seventy-two hours to get that done. The only problem was we had never tried remote working. A conversation with Jeff Schmitz, our CIO, to find out what it would take to quickly get our staff working from home by Monday morning yielded this response: "Are you out of your mind?" After his shock, he quickly pushed beyond can/can't thinking and directed our IT team towards a "What's it going to take?" mentality. As I expected, they made it happen and had everyone working from home by Monday, March 16th at 8:00 a.m.

Our organization has faced a number of crisis situations in the past—the terrorist attacks of 9/11, hurricanes, floods, lockouts, and more—so we have a pretty good toolbox to keep everyone's mind right. But this was different. Yes, attitude and mindset were critical, but this pandemic had global health and safety implications. Our teammates—the key to the Houston Texans "machine"—were scared, and rightly so. They feared the impact that the coronavirus would have on them, their families, and our community. Although I could not predict the effect of the virus on the economy, I reassured them that everyone's job was safe, which took that one fear off the table for everyone.

NFL Commissioner Roger Goodell was clear from the start of the pandemic that the season would start on time. The first step was free agency and we were very active. We picked up big-time play makers like Brandin Cooks, Randall Cobb, and David Johnson. We then turned to the NFL Draft where the league and the clubs did the previously unimaginable. For the first time in history the Draft was conducted 100 percent virtually and was distributed across numerous broadcast platforms, resulting in staggering viewership ratings. Clearly, America needed a distraction from the coronavirus.

As COVID-19 engulfed our region, the McNair Family and the Texans donated millions of dollars to help families in need. Our teammates, with the generous support of our sponsors, quickly launched a platform of education resources under the "Huddle at Home" umbrella for kids in public education who were at risk of falling behind because schools were closed due to the pandemic. We also supported frontline workers by delivering meals and inspirational messages from our ownership, players, coaches, and staff. I served as co-chair of the Greater Houston COVID-19 Recovery Fund, along with my good friend Tony Chase, CEO of ChaseSource LP. The fund raised over $17 million and immediately put those dollars to work for our city, helping struggling families meet the most basic needs.

As June rolled around and COVID-19 cases continued to rise, I had a sinking feeling that hosting our season as normal might not be a reality after all. In fact, I had started watching English Premier League matches being played without fans and started to embrace that we would need to prepare for a similar future. As I considered our beloved Texans fans, my attention turned to our season ticket members, Club seat members, Luxe members, sponsors, broadcast partners, and others who serve as the financial foundation that fuels our success. It was imperative that we pull them closer to us than ever before. Our staff began a concerted effort to reach out and express our compassion, empathy, and friendship. Our entire team had thousands of conversations to ask, "How are you? How's your family? How's your team?" And, importantly, "Is there anything we can do to help?" Our goal was to connect authentically and serve the people and organizations that had done so much for us in the past. As Basketball Hall of Fame coach John Wooden said, "Adversity does not build character, it reveals it."

We engaged our fans in various ways, creatively hosting community outreach and volunteer events. Our annual Texans Cares Volunteer Day, which encourages our fans to make an impact in the community as they work alongside Texans players, cheerleaders, our mascot TORO, and our staff, reached a record two million people across the region, an enormous increase from the usual twenty-five hundred, thanks to the virtual platform. Our annual Team Luncheon, a cherished annual tradition where we unveil our team to the community near the conclusion of training camp, also happened virtually due to COVID-19 restrictions. Undeterred, Emily Bruss and our Community Relations team crushed it as they took an event that normally reaches about six hundred rabid Texans fans and turned it into an engagement opportunity that impacted over fifteen thousand and raised over $100,000 for our Champions for Youth initiatives.

Throughout the summer, our team prepared for the coming football season in a manner consistent with how Commissioner Goodell laid it out—on time, as scheduled. Of course, no one knew exactly what would happen in the fall, but we enacted all of the preparation systems and processes we have had in place for the past two decades, with slight adjustments, to ensure we were ready to deliver our best gameday experience ever. To adapt to a "no fans" environment, our GEMS team (Game Entertainment Management System) got to work, along with Jay McDevitt and our digital team, to create a digital home for the array of rituals and traditions that make the Texans experience like none other in sports. We termed this our "Second Screen Experience" which was housed at the Game Day Central section of the Houston Texans app. It was a huge success, with great traffic, awesome engagement, and tremendous learnings for us as we work to enhance the at-home viewing experience for future seasons.

These are just some of the adjustments and innovations we enacted to navigate the coronavirus crisis, an unprecedented experience that swept the nation, the globe, and every business sector imaginable. Our actions during this adversity were not the keys to victory for us. They were actually the outcomes that facilitated our successful navigation of the choppy seas. I credit our success to the work that has been done over two decades, allowing us to successfully handle adversity. Although the coronavirus is still with us, we have made the very best of a bad situation by having the right attitude and a clear focus for the daily activities of our team. We started our season on time, we welcomed fans back to NRG Stadium, and we protected our "machine" through another crisis. Although 2020 was a year we would all like to forget, our organization emerged relatively unscathed and continued to fulfill our ambitions to win championships, create memorable experiences, and do great things for Houston.

In leadership, the real keys to victory during times of crisis and adversity come into focus. You cannot develop these behaviors during a crisis. By then it's too late. You're sunk. They must be cultivated during the good times.

★★★★★

Having worked for a number of years in Corporate America, I have a reasonable perspective on the differences between that environment and a sports franchise. At a normal job, most days, weeks, and even years are fairly consistent. However, in sports, especially the NFL, each season is a virtual roller coaster of emotions. Wins on Sunday bring incredible joy to our fans and ecstasy for everyone involved with the team. Conversely, losses might ruin the drive home for our season ticket members, but for those on the inside, the agony lasts at least until the next chance to compete. Because we have relatively few games each year compared to Major League Baseball, each game lost is like a ten-game losing streak over a three-hour window, and even worse with multiple losses in a row. It starts to feel like the whole world hates you. Even your dog doesn't want you around.

Sustained success in the NFL, sports, really anywhere, is highly contingent on keeping the environment inside the building constant, regardless of whether the outside world is tossing roses or throwing grenades your way. Having a specific playbook to manage both adversity and success has kept me and our organization centered. The foundation of navigating the highs and the lows lies in your attitude. It is both as simple and as hard as that.

## Four Plays to Handle Adversity

When confronted with adversity, accept the truth that life, especially leadership, is riddled with challenge. It's like a stick. If you pick one up, you get both ends. You have to fight through challenge on your leadership journey. It comes with the territory. Accept it, embrace it, then get about doing what must be done to overcome it. Dr. M. Scott Peck, in his book *The Road Less Traveled*, states, "Life is difficult. Once we truly understand and accept this truth, then life is no longer difficult." My home of Houston is filled with live oaks. They are bent and twisted as they find their way around all adversity. These beautiful trees serve as a great reminder to always look for ways to be flexible and adapt to the changing environment. Do so, and you might be able to bend your way around all of life's adversity.

When facing adversity, you must maintain situational awareness. This approach calls you to carefully define each environment you face, and not let your environment define you or your ability to respond. Responsible leadership, particularly in times of adversity, means always staying response-able. When you respond properly, you avoid any form of worry, because worry is like RPMs in an automobile. There is activity, but it doesn't get you anywhere. Handling adversity well requires you to discipline your thinking. As the leader, negative thoughts are an indulgence you cannot afford.

The four plays in my playbook to handle adversity address both the wins and the losses, the highs and the lows. In leadership, you are bound to have a healthy mix of both.

## Play #1: Push back

According to Barbara Corcoran—businesswoman, investor, and personality on the hit TV program *Shark Tank*—having the right attitude following a failure is key to success. "The most important trait you need as an entrepreneur is, when you take a hit, not to feel sorry for yourself," she says. "When you take a hit, bounce back." This is an essential insight for every leader.

Early in my sports career, I saw the power generated by a complete commitment to pushing back. That eventually successful effort changed the game of soccer in America forever. When I was with the Columbus Crew in Major League Soccer, we wanted to build a stadium for our team that would be the first of its kind in America. Actually, we thought a downtown stadium was part of the plan when the franchise was launched, but that plan fell victim to a referendum almost immediately. We looked at several other cities to serve as our home base, and eventually settled on Dublin, Ohio, feeling confident that we had the green light to move forward. Unfortunately, after a petition and another referendum, we were back at square one.

Feeling the sting of defeat, I left our post-election gathering and drove our owner Lamar Hunt to his hotel. The occasion called for a double Scotch from the hotel bar, but instead, we stopped at McDonald's for a Big Mac. While I ordered, Lamar walked over to a large map of Columbus displayed on the wall. "What are you doing?" I asked.

"I'm trying to figure out where we're going to put this stadium," he replied without taking his eyes off the map."

I was perplexed. Hadn't we just failed twice to get a stadium in the city of our choice? How many more defeats did this guy want? "You mean after two failed votes, we aren't moving?" I asked in frustration.

He shot back, "Now, why would we do that?" Lamar had decided to push back, and in that instant gave me the green light to do the same.

The next day, as I did numerous media interviews with local media to relay Lamar's commitment to find a solution in Columbus, my fax machine started spitting out offers and opportunities nonstop. Later that afternoon, I received a call from a top administrator for the state of Ohio saying he wanted to show me an underutilized plot of land owned by the state just outside of downtown Columbus. The site was perfect and had plenty of parking to accommodate us for the foreseeable future. The terms were fair, and soon we had laid the path for what would become the first soccer-specific stadium for an MLS franchise. This might sound simplistic, but that result happened because Lamar Hunt was committed to pushing back. Commitment is a powerful thing. A quote from the book *The Scottish Himalayan Expedition* by mountaineer William Hutchinson Murray says it best:

"Until one is committed, there is hesitancy, the chance to draw back, concerning all acts of initiative (and creation), there is one elementary truth that ignorance of which kills countless ideas and splendid plans: that the moment one definitely commits oneself, then Providence moves too. All sorts of things occur to help one that would never otherwise have occurred. A whole stream of events issues from the decision, raising in one's favor all manner of unforeseen incidents and meetings and material assistance, which no man could have dreamed would have come his way. Whatever you can do, or dream you can do, begin it. Boldness has genius, power, and magic in it. Begin it now."

I carried that quote with me throughout our quest for a stadium in Columbus and it brought me great strength and inspiration. It is on the wall of my office to this day. It reminds me of the imperative (Play #1) to always push back against adversity. It also reminds me of my hero, mentor, and friend, Lamar Hunt, who taught me this lesson through his attitude, passion, and conviction.

## Play #2: Stay positively focused

One of the key things I learned in sales training at IBM was the power of F.U.D.—Fear, Uncertainty, and Doubt. For a salesperson, F.U.D. can be one's best friend because the pain or risk of loss is a much more powerful motivator than an opportunity for gain. Of the three, I believe fear is the most powerful way to motivate humans.

In times of adversity, fear is your arch enemy. Fear distorts reality, engages the fight or flight response, and magnifies the risk of any adverse situation. It can cause you to take incorrect actions, or worse, paralyze you into inaction. When facing adversity, make a conscious choice to keep your mind alert and focused to ensure that those you lead do the same. You must bring forward the courage to act.

IBM chairman and CEO Thomas Watson once said of attacking challenges ferociously, "Solve it. Solve it quickly. Solve it right or wrong. If you solve it wrong, it will come back and slap you in the face, and then you can solve it right. Lying dead in the water and doing nothing is a comfortable alternative because it is without risk, but it is an absolutely fatal way to manage a business." And, I might add, it is particularly destructive in times of adversity. This truth has stuck with me throughout my leadership journey and it has been particularly helpful during times of adversity. It speaks to the need to have a predisposition for action.

As the antidote to this, the concept of being positively focused crystallized for the Texans in 2011 when we faced the potential for a work stoppage in the NFL. There were discussions between the NFL Management Council (the League) and the Players Association (the Union). The two sides were so far apart they seemed to be speaking different languages. It was January, and despite the acrimony between the League and the players, at the team level, we needed to address our mentality in order to maximize prospects for an optimal outcome. We decided that our best option was to remain positively focused. That entailed a number of options for the well-being of our staff. We made the decision not consider furloughs, layoffs, or other extreme measures to anticipate what might happen during the off season. This gave our teammates security that their jobs were protected so they could focus on the important work at hand.

We reminded our teammates to look for the positives that existed, since by all appearances, the media would not. Media outlets benefit from the fear that comes from chaotic events. Therefore, we needed to dial back from what we saw, heard, and read to maintain a more balanced and positive view. More importantly, we had to steel ourselves to resist the natural temptation to fixate on things we couldn't influence, and instead focus solely on what we could control. Stephen Covey, in his best-selling book, *The Seven Habits of Highly Effective People*®, addresses the circle of influence and the typically much larger circle of concern. In general, time spent in your circle of concern shrinks your circle of influence. Conversely, a relentless focus on your circle of influence causes it to expand until it eventually overlaps your circle of concern. At that point, you have the power to influence all that concerns you. Consciously fixate on controlling the control-ables and let everything else go.

As important as it is to stay focused on what you *can* control, it is even more important to consciously and intentionally reject what you *can't* control. You probably have never heard of Mark Owen, but I bet you have heard of Osama bin Laden. Mark was a Navy SEAL on the bin Laden raid and spoke to our teammates a few years back. He told us that, as the Navy SEALs flew back from the raid, he was on headset with the pilots. They were concerned about not being able to make it back safely. In the end, they did, but at that moment, with all of the fear-filled chatter (justified as it might have been), Mark unplugged his headset. He knew there was nothing he could do. If you can't control the chaos, you have to discipline yourself to unplug.

Lastly, we committed to being totally transparent with the staff. Especially in crisis, any vacuum of communication is naturally filled with negativity and cynicism. Our leadership team met regularly with our teammates to tell them everything we knew and to answer their questions to the best of our ability. This open dialogue built trust, which allowed all of our teammates to remain positively focused on preparing for the season to begin on time, as scheduled. They could trust that they would never be surprised by bad news.

When the new collective bargaining agreement was ratified in July and we began our season as originally contemplated, the positively focused mindset was vindicated and it became part of our toolkit for future use. I'd like to believe that the way we handled that level of adversity, and the mindset that all our teammates maintained throughout the process, had some influence on the Houston Texans experiencing our most successful performance on record.

## Play #3: Believe

Have you ever heard the story of a young man who was fired early in his career for lacking imagination and having no original ideas? Not a ringing endorsement for any aspiring leader, especially someone who would go on to redefine entertainment as we know it today. That young man was none other than Walter Elias Disney. According to Walt, "Faith is the most important thing. If you believe in something, believe it 'til the end, unequivocally and without hesitation." This faithful spirit, the ability to believe without seeing, is what allowed Walt Disney to build what remains today the most admired entertainment organization on the planet. Walt faced extreme adversity throughout this career. In fact, once Disneyland launched and became a success, he commented, "I could never convince the financiers that Disneyland was feasible because dreams offer too little collateral." But he never lost his commitment nor his belief in fulfillment of the ideas that he faithfully championed. For all of us who love the many entertainment offerings that Disney produces, we have been blessed by his ability to believe.

The designation of a "doubting Thomas" comes from the biblical story of St. Thomas, one of Jesus' twelve disciples. As the story goes, Thomas would not believe in the risen Christ without definitive, physical evidence. Essentially, Jesus invited Thomas to poke his finger into the wound left in Jesus' side after his violent crucifixion. Once Thomas saw the proof, he believed. But, here's the kicker, Jesus said, "Blessed are those who have not seen, and yet believe." Ouch! Although the context of the modern working world is different than what Jesus faced, the concept is the same. The ability to believe in a positive outcome, despite the adversity you face, is both powerful and essential for you as a leader. Moreover, your ability to inspire others to believe is fundamental to your ability to lead others through crisis.

The willingness to believe without seeing is powerfully summed up by Rosabeth Moss Kanter in her book *Confidence: How Winning and Losing Streaks Begin and End.* "Everything looks like failure in the middle." When you do big things, great things, you will face adversity. When you do, you have to wholeheartedly believe in your eventual success and you must inspire others to do the same. Blessed are those who have not seen, yet still believe.

## Play #4: Persevere

Dr. Kanter made another important observation at the end of *Confidence*, which speaks to the critical nature of a commitment to persevere in the face of adversity: "The difference between winning and losing is so often how long people give it before they give up." Perseverance is the raw gumption to keep going even when things look dismal. The will to persevere through adversity comes from a hidden place deep inside each of us. It doesn't reveal itself on a daily basis. You might not even know it's there. But when you need it, that place of perseverance reveals itself. The thing is, you have to answer the call and allow it to rise up inside of you. You must allow it to overtake every bit of F.U.D. you can imagine, and just keep on keeping on.

In the book *Shut Up and Listen!* by my friend Tilman Fertitta, he states very plainly the business imperative to persevere: "You're not out of business until you don't have the last dollar to go out and buy product to make, until somebody comes and padlocks your door, or you can't make payroll." This exemplifies the sheer perseverance and determination to keep going no matter what. "Never give in. Never, never, never," said Winston Churchill in his address to the Harrow School in London. "In nothing great or small, large or petty, never give in, except to convictions of honor and good sense. Never yield to force. Never yield to the apparently overwhelming might of the enemy." Churchill's mindset changed the face of our modern world for the better. Achieving great things is not easy. Success does not always go to the biggest, the fastest, or the strongest, but so often simply to the last one standing. Always endeavor to be that one.

To help me and my team remember the need to always keep fighting, I use a line from the movie *The Best Exotic Marigold Hotel*, which I saw by accident on a red-eye flight back to Houston. In the movie, Sonny the innkeeper said, "Everything will be all right in the end, and if it is not all right, it is not yet the end." This quote provides a mindset that allows you to peacefully and confidently persevere through adversity. I encourage you to call these four plays often when adversity strikes. That's what leaders do.

Adversity must be accepted and expected along your journey to achieve great things. Attitude is your secret weapon when you and your team face adversity. Author and motivational speaker Dr. Wayne Dyer effectively summed up the power of a positive attitude when he said, "Change the way you look at things, and the things you look at change." That's easy to say when you have a few minor issues to deal with. But life as a leader can be tough. Throw in family obligations, and it has the potential to be overwhelming. One tool I use often in challenging times is what I call the blessings and burdens exercise. It is simple, and it keeps your mind right and your focus on the most important tasks at hand.

Scan the QR code to receive a Bonus PDF Blessings & Burdens

**Step 1:** Take a piece of paper and draw a line down the middle. Label the top left "blessings" and the top right "burdens."

**Step 2:** Off the top of your head, write down all the things you are thankful for in your life on the left side of the page. I usually list health, my beautiful wife and amazing kids, a great job, and several other things.

**Step 3:** List all of the major challenges you are currently facing on the right side of the page. I usually only come up with three to five, which in itself is instantly cathartic because the blessings far outweigh the burdens.

**Step 4:** Review all of the burdens listed and define the action steps you can take right away to make progress against them.

That's your to-do list for tomorrow.

Please try it. I hope it brings you peace of mind and a balanced perspective on your life, regardless of the adversities you face.

★★★★★

One winter I went out for a run at 6:00 a.m. and I found myself ruminating over negative thoughts regarding challenges the coming off-season would pose for us. When I got back to the house, I wrote down all the things I was thankful for in my life. A beautiful, loving wife, two great kids, an amazing neighborhood. You get the picture. In minutes, I had written fifteen reasons to be grateful. Then, I listed the burdens in my life, of which there were three. I smiled, then created an action plan to resolve the burdens I was facing. As I often say, a well-defined problem is half solved. The blessings and burdens exercise is an exceptional tool for creating the energy and the focus to solve life's ever-present challenges.

## Four Plays to Handle Success

I've worked with many amazing professionals in this industry. Among the best is Dom Capers, the original head coach of the Houston Texans. Among the most memorable of his notable sayings is, "For every ten players that can handle adversity, there's only one that can handle success." Similarly, my good friend and NFL alum, Spencer Tillman likes to say, "It's hard to run with a full cup of success." And I believe it.

Handling adversity is hard. Handling success is even harder. Adversity provides a clear and present danger. You know you're in trouble and you do what you can to figure a way out or through it. But success is the silent assassin. You don't know you're in trouble, but you definitely are. I believe that the challenge of handling success can be boiled down to one word that defines a very natural human tendency when things go well—hubris. Excessive pride or self-confidence is your invisible enemy. Fortunately, there are four plays you can call on to handle success.

## Play #1: Stay humble

*Shark Tank*'s Barbara Corcoran nailed this one when she said, "The main mistake small business owners make is getting caught up in vanity." I believe that actually applies to all of us. Fortunately, there is an antidote for vanity. It is a commitment to stay humble.

Lamar Hunt was likely the most humble man I have ever met. His humility served him very well. When I worked for him at the Columbus Crew, he would always fly coach when he came to visit. Despite his great wealth, he remained incredibly humble, worked hard every day, and showed genuine concern for the well-being of others. That is why his friend, Jack Steadman ended his remarks at the funeral service for Lamar by stating, "When God made man, he had Lamar Hunt in mind."

Melissa and I got married in 1998. My only job in the wedding planning process was to find the honeymoon location. We were strapped for cash, so I found the cheapest room possible at an all-inclusive resort in Jamaica. When we arrived at the hotel, an agent greeted us and accompanied us to a private bungalow with champagne, music, and other VIP amenities. A few minutes later, the concierge called to inform us that we would be escorted to our private villa on the beach. Like an idiot, I said, "That's not right. We can't afford that!"

The concierge calmly replied, "Mr. and Mrs. Rootes, you have been upgraded. The benefactor asked that we not reveal their name." He never said a word about it, but it had to have been Lamar Hunt who transformed a good honeymoon into a legendary experience for me and my bride.

When I left the Columbus Crew to join the Houston Texans, Lamar was surprised and not entirely happy with the move. Our soccer stadium had recently opened, our future was incredibly bright, and now Lamar would have to find another leader for the organization. When I saw Lamar at my first NFL owner's meeting, he made a bee line for me. He shook my hand and left in it a keychain emblazoned with the name Melissa, that I am pretty sure he had bought in the hotel gift shop. That was his way of saying we were okay, which brought tears to my eyes. Why would someone of his stature care about his relationship with a thirty-something sports executive? It was because he appreciated and respected everyone in his world. His example of humility has been an incredible blessing and inspiration to me.

## Play #2: Stay focused

Success is simply a distraction that threatens to derail your future achievements. Coach Capers called it the "poison pill of success" that you have to resist swallowing at all costs. To counteract its effects, you have to identify the habits that have made you successful and stay laser focused on them in order to reach beyond success to excellence. According to Aristotle, "We are what we repeatedly do. Excellence, therefore, is not an act, but a habit." Once you achieve success, you must focus to counteract the natural distractions that come with it. To sustain success, you must focus on your success habits.

After Houston Texans defensive lineman J.J. Watt signed his landmark $100 million contract, he texted a picture of himself in the weight room at 4:00 a.m. the next day with the caption, "This is how I am going to respond to getting paid." He was demonstrating what his focused commitment to success would look like. In our Deep

Steel Blue conference room at NRG Stadium (yes, our conference rooms are named after our team colors), there is a quote on the wall from J.J.: "Success is not owned, it's leased, and rent is due every day." That is the mindset that has allowed J.J. to become one of the greatest athletes of all time in any sport.

You and your team must always fight the temptation to focus on your success rather than your success habits. Develop a way of doing things, clearly articulate it, and make sure everyone remains committed to it so you can avoid the distraction of success.

## Play #3: Stay balanced

Fortunately, I've always had outstanding role models, like Lamar Hunt and Bob McNair. They taught me that a successful life is not a sprint, it's a marathon. Demands of the day can take you out of balance. For example, consistently working 18-hour days can threaten the stability of your marriage and your performance as a parent. Likewise, spend too long away from work, and your business influence fades. The key is balance. Maintaining balance requires that you regularly make appropriate deposits into each of the buckets (roles) that matter in your life. Early in my career, I was consumed with my work and regularly put in ridiculous hours most days of the week to achieve business success. That type of imbalance is not sustainable over time. Eventually, I needed to recharge to avoid burnout, health challenges, or worse.

One of the best professional experiences I have ever had has been my membership in Young President's Organization (YPO), a global community of thirty thousand chief executives in more than one hundred, thirty countries. Once in YPO, I was assigned to a forum that consisted of nine other presidents of leading Houston businesses who became my personal board of directors and dear friends. We met monthly for four hours and the foundation of the meeting was a 5-minute confidential update from each member. We covered three areas: business, family, and personal. This forum was helpful for me for many reasons, most importantly, the monthly updates kept me accountable for staying balanced. I not only became a better leader, but also a better husband and father because I knew each month I had to face my friends and discuss my progress. I also had to think deeply about what mattered most to me. Once that was on the table, my forum mates were there to hold me accountable for pursuing those priorities.

Staying balanced, in Stephen Covey's "put first things first" parlance, is important but not urgent. You can ignore it and put it off. But if you do, it will eventually catch up to you. You can succeed without balance, but the only way to achieve long-term, sustained success is to maintain a balanced focus on the business, family, and personal priorities in your life. Or, as C. S. Lewis said, "Put first things first and second things are thrown in. Put second things first and you lose both first and second things."

Another tool I use as a weapon to protect the priorities I hold most dear is my calendar. Often, I've had an invitation to attend an event, and I wanted to decline but I knew it wouldn't go over well. I would check my calendar, praying that I had a conflict. If I didn't, I would accept the invitation. If, however, I already had time blocked for business, family, or personal priorities, I would feel confident to decline. This can only happen with an updated, well-managed calendar. Proactively reserving time on your calendar to address your priorities is critical to staying balanced. Carve out time each month to maintain calendar. Doing so increases your chances of nurturing balance in your life and allows you the stability to maximize your success indefinitely.

## Play #4: Go forward

Once you are on a successful path, evaluate your goals periodically and reset to keep yourself motivated. High expectations are powerful motivators for individuals and organizations.

Golfer Rory McIlroy serves as a terrific example of the forward mindset. Despite his immense success, he always pushes for more. This attitude helps him avoid the Sunday nerves, which must come with leading a tournament. His approach is, "If I'm two ahead going into the weekend, I'm going to try to get three ahead. And if I'm three ahead, I'm going to try to get four ahead. I'm just going to try to keep the pedal down and get as many ahead as possible. That is my mindset whenever I'm leading the tournament."

The "go forward" mindset demands that you constantly challenge yourself to be even better. As the saying goes, "You are either getting better or you're getting worse. Nothing ever stays the same." To ensure you are not degrading, focus on improvement. Believe it or not, success is a distraction that has the potential to put a ceiling on your achievement. To be your very best self, reject the spoils of success and focus on getting even better. You may never earn a green jacket, hoist a trophy, or represent as part of the Ryder Cup team, but you do face the same distractions that come with success on the golf course, the gridiron, or the diamond. Commit to going forward to avoid swallowing the poison pill of success.

Handling adversity and success require discipline to maintain correct attitudes by controlling your thoughts. "Carefully watch your thoughts, for they become your words," Gandhi said. "Manage and watch your words, for they will become your actions. Consider and judge your actions, for they have become your habits. Acknowledge and watch your habits, for they shall become your values. Understand and embrace your values, for they become your destiny."

Indeed, your thoughts define your destiny. As a leader, you need to model and correct your thinking, whether you are winning or losing at the present time. Like national championship winning Notre Dame coach Lou Holtz said, "Winners and losers aren't born. They are products of how they think." Play to win!

# CHAPTER 6

# Your Leadership Playbook

O ver my lifetime of studying leadership, I have gained an immense amount of clarity regarding the key talents that exceptional leaders must master. These characteristics and behaviors come naturally for very few people. Most, like myself, have to work to master them. The daily practice of being aware of these traits and intentionally enacting them in every interaction is a job unto itself. This is one reason that being an effective leader requires a lifetime of practice.

During my leadership journey, I've developed an acronym, P.R.A.I.S.E., which reminds me of the key talents in which I need to excel.

## People-focused

A team never out-performs its talent level. Great leaders know that, and now, you do too. Make sure you have the right players in the right positions, always. Great leaders work exceptionally well with all people because they are able to influence.

During one of many all-nighters while at Procter & Gamble, I worked on a marketing campaign. One of our product category leaders stopped by my desk and asked what I was working on. When I told her, she shared a story about a similar campaign she had led that was wildly successful. A broad smile crossed her face and her eyes lit up. I could sense the pride emanating from her. Then, looking off into the distance, she said, "You're so lucky. You get to work with things. I have to work with people." Suddenly, that prideful smile was gone. She added, "People suck." She didn't last long in her leadership role.

As you rise in an organization, your functional expertise becomes less important. Your ability to do *things* becomes secondary to your ability to do *people*. Real leaders know how to influence people.

## Resilient

Failure in life is unavoidable. Failure as a leader is inevitable. The ability to quickly bounce back from failure is a strength you must develop as you grow into leadership. Learn to view failure the way inventor Thomas Edison did. "I have not failed. I've just found ten thousand ways that won't work," he famously said. When you do big things that are important, sometimes it doesn't work out. Failure isn't final, as long as you maintain the right attitude.

While hosting a major international soccer match between A. C. Milan and Chivas Guadalajara at NRG Stadium, our Texans staff was in for a surprise. The game came together late, so we knew we wouldn't have a large crowd. What we didn't know was that we were in store for a comedy of errors regarding the installation of a temporary grass field. The first problem was our groundskeeper took a different job a month prior to the game, which left us without the expertise required to handle the issues that inevitably come up. Second, the sod we received was not of high quality. After the sod installation, we needed to put sand in the seams to prepare the field for the game, but for some reason, we did not have any green sand onsite. The operations crew—without oversight of an agronomist—used white sand, which only highlighted the seams and other imperfections in the field. It looked like a cow pasture! All of this nearly caused the game to be cancelled, which would have been both costly and embarrassing. The match eventually was played, but in all honesty, it wasn't a shining moment for our sister company, Lone Star Sports & Entertainment, of which I am the founder and president. After the match, I felt humiliated. Even Houston's mayor commented to me the next day, "What the heck happened with your field?" At that point, I was reminded of something former U.S. Men's National Soccer Team coach Bora Milutinović once said to me, "What is the most important one? The next one!"

It was late July and we had experienced a setback, but I knew we had another major event on the horizon, the Texas Kickoff Classic featuring LSU and Wisconsin during Labor Day weekend. I quickly turned all of our organization's focus towards making this event the best we had ever produced on every metric. To inspire our team, I often used a quote from Rosabeth Moss Kanter's book *Confidence*. "How do you avoid a losing streak? Never lose two times in a row." We had lost, but we had to win this next one at all costs, whatever it took. I also reminded our team to not turn one mistake into two by dwelling on our setback. Our complete focus on going forward and not being defined by our past failure led us to produce the largest college football crowd in NRG Stadium history and an event that will long be remembered as a game for the ages.

## Authentic

For exceptional leaders, work isn't labor, it's a calling. If you haven't experienced this yet, keep rising and you'll see. At their core, great leaders believe that what they and their team do is big and it matters.

It's part of who they are. Like the chorus from Kathy Mattea's song, *Come From the Heart*, "It's gotta come from the heart if you want it to work." That heart work is the passion you exude.

Having a passion for your organization's mission illustrates your authentic desire to walk the talk and to encourage others to do the same. When you are straightforward with your teammates, you demonstrate an authentic honesty and simplicity that becomes sticky and that others want to mirror. Beyond all of the accolades, the results, and the outcomes, your role as an authentic leader should matter to you down to the core of who you are. As IBM founder, Thomas Watson put it, "To be successful, you have to have your heart in your business and your business in your heart." This applies double for leaders.

## Inspiring

Leaders are always, always, ALWAYS on stage. Everything you do, everything you say, every word you write is evaluated for its meaning for the team. That is an incredible burden, but it is also an amazing opportunity when you embrace it with everything you do.

By publicly recognizing and appreciating the efforts of your team, you inspire them to do more, reach higher, try harder, and support each other. There are always detractors of recognition programs because not everyone gets a trophy. But I know of no better way to encourage behavior than to recognize it. More broadly, inspiring a team involves lifting everyone's sights beyond individual desires to what the team wants. This comes back to the core purpose of the organization. Everyone wants to do something big that matters. What is that for your organization? Focus everyone's sights on that and you'll be surprised at the results you see.

## See around corners

Seeing around corners means anticipating the disruptions which might derail your plans. Kodak and Blockbuster are two examples of successful businesses that needed to see around the corners and prepare to successfully navigate disruption. You don't have to predict the future, you just need to pay attention to the trends that require action in order to maintain a growth trajectory. When exceptional leaders are authentically engaged in the work of the organization, they develop an intuitive feel for the opportunities and threats that exist over the horizon. They see things before others do. This is because they spend their time working *on* the business rather than *in* the business. Therefore, embrace this imperative. Lean in to your role to be the captain charting the course.

## Execution

Without a process that gets things done, none of the previous talents or characteristics matter. You establish a direction that everyone embraces. You communicate in a clear, consistent, and motivational fashion to push your team forward. Without a process—a way to ensure things get done—you are doomed to underperform. Execution brings together the who, the how, and the why of your organization's mission and culture. Great people, strong culture, and a compelling purpose put strategy into action for incredible results. But what would happen if you had an execution system that paired strategy with the right people, a great culture, and a compelling purpose? That should be the goal of your leadership journey.

At the Texans, we use a rigorous goal-setting and planning protocol, monthly priorities, quarterly reviews, and other systems to ensure we stay on track towards exceptional results each year. We use STEP (Success Through Excellent Planning), GEMS (Game

Entertainment Management System), and other processes to ensure that our most important activities are meticulously managed. If it is important, you can be sure that there is a "Texans Way" of doing it.

# Leading Change

Leadership and change go hand in hand. Leaders help the group they represent grow from one state of being to a more desirable state. Leading a change effort requires specific dynamics in order to maximize the outcomes of change. When the opportunity for change arises, sometimes during a crisis, you have to create a sense of urgency. Rarely is change something that can wait. This isn't to suggest that every change opportunity is an emergency, but the very nature of change requires immediate attention, if not also quick, decisive action. When making change requires the action of your teammates—and it almost always does—you have to demonstrate the reason the change is necessary and beneficial. You must get buy-in by creating and communicating the vision for change. You have to make steady progress, and persist until the expected change is realized.

If I asked you to throw this book out of the window right now, would you? Wait, don't answer that! But seriously, if I told you to do something that you thought was extreme, we would probably need considerable back and forth, and then you still may not take the action I requested. However, if I brought my good friend F.U.D. over (Fear, Uncertainty, and Doubt), I'd have a pretty good chance of getting your tail in gear, no matter how outlandish the request. Motivating your team in the direction of the starting block of change requires that you reveal the burning platform—the compelling reason—to take action towards growth.

In Stephen Covey's book *The Seven Habits of Highly Effective People®*, he relays the story of Captain Horatio Hornblower. As the story goes, one night at sea, Horatio awakens to find that a ship is in his sea lane, about twenty miles away, and refuses to move. Horatio commands the other ship to move starboard, twenty degrees at once. The other ship refuses and tells Horatio that he should move his ship starboard twenty degrees at once. Next, Horatio tries to pull rank and size on the other ship, stating that he's a captain and that he's on a large battle ship. The other ship replies, I'm a lighthouse. Until Captain Hornblower saw clearly that there was a compelling reason to change, a change was not on the table. Once he saw the light, he got in line. The first step in affecting change is to unequivocally establish that refusing to change is not a viable option.

In most organizations, change doesn't happen by the efforts of one person. It takes a village. As a leader, you want the concerted effort of your team to affect change. The results of a collaborative team effort are likely guarded and sustained by the team, thereby creating a long-term impact. Therefore, in order for any significant change effort to succeed, establish a committed coalition of advocates, maybe as many as 70 percent of your team, as early as possible in the effort. Get your team on board by creating a clear and inspiring vision of the future that they embrace. Show them a future that is worth the blood, sweat, and tears to bring it into reality. Drive the vision into their minds and hearts so *your* vision becomes *theirs*. The key to this is simplicity. A simple and compelling plan, well communicated and executed, beats a complex genius strategy all day long. And remember, communication is not what you say, but what is heard, remembered, and acted upon. That's the leader's communication standard.

By celebrating quick wins, you increase the existing commitment and enthusiasm of those who have bought in, and you build momentum. The size of the win doesn't matter.

Just show progress and celebrate it. Winning is freaking contagious! Demonstrating any level of tangible success encourages converts. At the end of the day, no one wants to be on the losing team when time expires. Potential winners don't want to be standing on the sidelines wishing they had been part of the win. Nothing converts doubters like putting points on the board. And nothing adds points to the board like persistent action. Moving forward, even when everything around you looks like failure, is critical in motivating your team towards a win. Believe in the change you're making and inspire your team to keep going. After all, the final win is theirs, too. Change can be hard in any organization, even when you face clear and present danger. Keep moving towards the finish line. The rewards of a hard-fought victory for change are immeasurable.

# Creativity/Cash = Excellence

In 2019, the prestigious Business Roundtable formally recognized for the first time something that I have always believed. In fact, their revelation is one of the foundational premises of this book: Business is more than profit. I adopted this belief after reading the book *The Goal: A Process of Ongoing Improvement* by Eliyahu M. Goldratt and Jeff Cox during my graduate school experience at Indiana University. "So this is the goal: To make money by increasing net profit, while simultaneously increasing return on investment, and simultaneously increasing cash flow."

I thought, "That's not the goal at all. Profit is merely a means to an end, the fuel that allows an organization to fulfill its purpose in the world." Not a very popular point of view at a respected business school in 1992, but I believed it. I have always held firm to the belief that profit is a reward that is to be distributed fairly to all of an organization's stakeholders. When that profit is shared, excellence is achieved. Leaders have the obligation to allocate profits appropriately to satisfy a variety of constituents, who include: 1) owners, who should be adequately rewarded for their capital investment and the risk they have taken; 2) employees, who should be recognized for their contribution to the organization's success; 3) customers, who should be provided exceptional value and recognition for their loyalty (This usually takes the form of reinvestments to improve the quality of the product or service.); and 4) community, which should benefit from the presence of the business, demonstrated through a variety of community support initiatives.

With this approach, every dollar within a business is allocated, either consciously or unconsciously, to various stakeholders. Any dollar spent beyond what is absolutely required comes at the expense of the company's entire ecosystem of stakeholders. In essence, it is wasted. Owners, employees, customers, and the community are short-changed by any unnecessary spending. That's where the concept of creativity over cash comes in.

When launching the Columbus Crew in Major League Soccer, I befriended the leader of an improvisational performance group. I learned a lot from him, most importantly the concept of creativity over cash. Most people believe problems can be solved by money alone. The reality is, creativity and human ingenuity can often solve problems for pennies on the dollar. Don't get me wrong, there's no advantage to doing things on the cheap. Great leaders always challenge their team to find solutions that are not only effective, but also executed with maximum efficiency. The eloquent yet simple motto of Benjamin Franklin, "A penny saved is a penny earned," still rings true in business today. Pennies saved through addressing the day-to-day problems in business as cost-effectively as possible can be reinvested in customers, employees, and the community, or returned to the owners. All it takes is a little creativity/cash.

In the first year of the Columbus Crew, we trained on the campus of The Ohio State University. We used the locker room at Ohio Stadium as our changing room and we practiced on the intramural fields. Not the ideal setup for a major league sports franchise, but this was a startup and we were operating with the thinnest of margins. The goal was not to make a profit, but to lose as little as possible during our early days. One night, while watching the news, I saw a story about my team and what had happened that day. The intramural fields were locked and our players had to scale a high fence to get to practice! I decided at that moment, enough was enough. I knew an impassioned plea to Lamar Hunt to build a training complex would only encourage him to drug test me because to him I obviously would have had to be high to make such an outlandish and unreasonable request. Instead I employed creativity/cash.

I reconnected with a development official from the city of Obetz, just south of Columbus, who I had met by chance months earlier at an event. I shared our practice facility challenges and I could see his wheels turning. He knew of a tract of land he believed would be perfect as a practice facility. Better still, he was confident he could make the case for the positive economic development benefits of the Columbus Crew taking up residence in Obetz to higher-ups in the city government. In the end, we signed a long-term lease on two practice fields and a training facility, custom designed for us and exclusively reserved for our use, all at a cost comparable to what we were paying at The Ohio State. It also was the first training facility built for a Major League Soccer franchise and it gave our players the respect and sense of permanence they deserved.

Anybody can write a check, assuming they have the funds to cover it. Sometimes money is an integral part of a solution. More often than not, employing a little creativity/cash can help you achieve what is required to move the business forward and maintain your financial resources to reward your owners, recognize your employees, value your customers, and serve your community.

# Lead From the Bottom Up

A winning game plan can be initiated both top down and bottom up. Just like in your four-dimensional leadership view, you have to operate within your game plan knowing that your *responsibilities* to others are as important as your *responsibility* to them. This leadership thing is truly a team effort. Maintaining a trust-based pact that all participants steadfastly protect is critical in order to have the most productive relationship and outcomes possible. Lead that trust and you will experience incredible growth in your role as a leader.

At the end of 2018, my hero, role model, and dear friend Bob McNair lost his courageous battle with cancer. After working directly for Bob for nearly twenty years, I would now report to his son, Cal. I had known Cal for almost as long as I had known Bob. However, we had nowhere near the shared experiences and track record together as I'd had with Bob. Essentially, I was starting over with building trust with my boss. I desperately wanted to get off to a fast start and enjoy the trusting partnership I'd enjoyed with Bob McNair for so long.

One Saturday morning, I awoke early with something weighing on my mind. I found myself coming up with things that were vital in my relationship with Bob and kept thinking, "Geez, I wish Cal knew that." During my morning run, things started to crystallize for me. I decided to create a one-page "Things Cal needs to know" document that would form the foundation of our partnership. My hope was that this would allow us to get off to a fast start. Think about it, would anyone be stupid enough to communicate their own trust-related behavioral expectations to the team owner, in writing, unless they were absolutely committed to always meeting those expectations?

I wanted Cal to know that I would always have his back, just like I had Bob's. My role as president of the Texans encompasses leading and inspiring our team to be and do their best, and I had to exemplify that to the new owner. My loyalty is to Cal and the organization and it is my responsibility to translate the Houston Texans vision into a plan our entire team will embrace and execute. In doing so, I assured him that I would be transparent with him and never blindside him with bad news, but rather give it to him early and completely. I shared that his outreach to me—whether a phone call, email, or text—would become my top priority. Although my role is to guide the day-to-day operations of the business, the teamwork he and I would share would be critical to the success of the business. Therefore, I would always offer my honest and candid assessment, advice, and counsel to help us arrive at the best decision for the team.

Trust, I assured him, would be our most important asset as partners. I let him know that I consider it an honor to work for him and his family. My focus, as it had always been, is on maintaining an eminently respected enterprise, and creating value for the McNair family, our Limited Partners, teammates, fans, and community. I let Cal know that he would have the same intense loyalty that his dad always had from me. Communicating and demonstrating that kind of leadership, bottom up, was important for us. That is a critical demonstration of how leaders play to win.

# CHAPTER 7

# Play to Win

It is noon on Saturday, October 3rd as I write these words. Our team is 0 - 3 having lost to the league champion Kansas City Chiefs, Baltimore Ravens, and Pittsburgh Steelers. Talk about a "murderer's row" to start the season!

I have put our playbook for handling adversity to good use over the past three weeks. I have reminded everyone we started 0 - 3 two years ago and needed five quarters (the game went into overtime after we squandered a big lead) and a questionable call by the Colts on fourth down to get into the win column. That one win set us up for a ten-game winning streak, another divisional title, and another home playoff game. Winning in this league is tough, and it all starts with believing. Just because you think you can win doesn't mean you will, but without belief and conviction in your heart you have no shot.

Off the field, our team is preparing to host fans at NRG Stadium for the first time in 2020. It will be great to see our home-field advantage again, even if we can only accommodate about eleven thousand fans due to social distancing requirements related to the coronavirus. Our first home game of the season against the Baltimore Ravens was played without fans and was a surreal experience. After eighteen consecutive seasons of sold-out crowds with over seventy thousand of the best fans in the NFL, we played a made-for-TV game and NRG Stadium served as the soundstage. Fortunately, tomorrow will provide some sense of normalcy for us, our fans, and our community.

We all have a responsibility to get this right so others can replicate our success model. Our team has done a terrific job in our preparations and I just sent the following note to them:

**From:** Jamey Rootes
**Date:** October 3, 2020 at 11:34:50 AM CDT
**To:** Karissa Hudik, Cody Disbennet, Holly Schweitzer, John Schriever, Suzie Thomas, Trey Young
**Subject:** Tomorrow
To: The *A Team*

I am in awe of the amazing job you all have done getting us ready to host fans at our games this season, despite the tremendous challenges involved. I am so proud of you and our organization and I hope you will take a few minutes tomorrow to step back and appreciate what a huge achievement you have orchestrated. Please let me know if there is anything I can do to support you. Otherwise, know I am having a hard time typing this note because of the tears in my eyes. That is the depth of the appreciation I have for you and the job you have so expertly done. Finish strong!

JR

P.S. - If you know of others who made significant contributions to our months of preparation, please forward this note to them with my apologies for my oversight. Please copy me so I am aware of these other impact players. #Respect

★★★★★

I could close by summarizing some of the essential elements of the Winning Game Plan formula. But you've already read the book and recapping would be redundantly redundant. Instead, I'll share three thoughts I believe are essential to your success. These may be the two most important concepts in this book. You might be thinking, "If these ideas are so important, why did you wait until the last chapter to reveal them?" That's a good question. You, my friend, have invested your time to make it to the end of this book and that type of commitment should be rewarded. Expect, inspect, and reward, right? Those who fail to demonstrate your perseverance will miss out, giving you an advantage. And an advantage is only an advantage if you take advantage of it. Given your determination to be great, I bet taking advantage of your newfound knowledge and understanding is exactly what you'll do. So, without further adieu, here are the three essential things I believe you need to be if you want to have consistent success:

## Be an optimist

When you accept the role of leader, negative thoughts become a luxury you can no longer afford. They are an indulgence and a distraction. You have to control the natural thoughts of fear, insecurity, and defeat that arise within you.

Bob McNair said it best during an interview with Marc Vandermeer, the voice of the Texans. Marc asked Bob, "You are always so positive. Why is that?"

Bob instantly responded, "Have you ever seen a successful person who wasn't?"

Coach Vince Lombardi's best quote of all time applies doubly for leaders: "You better be fired with enthusiasm or you will be fired with enthusiasm." Your team needs you to bring the juice every day, all the time. Some will criticize you and call you myopic at the start. God knows they criticized my energy, enthusiasm, and positivity and said I was naive as the 29-year-old general manager of the Columbus Crew. In fact, after our logo launch for the Crew, *Columbus Monthly* magazine mocked me and the Brooks Brothers suit my "Mommy" bought me. They also quoted another sports team owner as saying, "They won't draw eighteen thousand fans. They will be lucky to get eighteen hundred." Yes, bulletin board material applies off the field, too. As a leader, you will never receive blessings (or business results) beyond your ability to believe.

I have read *The Power of Positive Thinking* by Dr. Norman Vincent Peale thousands of times to develop my optimism. Literally, thousands of times. I have committed numerous passages to memory so they are available to me at all times and in all situations I face. That takes me to my second key concept.

## Be an "over-learner"

While reading this book, you might have thought, "Why does this guy use so many acronyms?" Another good question! There is a method to the madness. Acronyms are my primary method for over-learning important concepts. When I find an idea or model I believe to be effective, I turn it into an acronym and typically post it somewhere in my office. I refer to it often to drill it into my conscious mind, and eventually into my subconscious mind. Once it gets into my subconscious mind, it becomes instantly available to me as situations arise. These tools flow to me when needed, almost like a guardian angel.

I use quotes in a similar fashion and I am a meticulous note taker. Benjamin Franklin said, "I would advise you to read with a pen in hand, and enter in a little book short hints of what you find that is curious, or that may be useful; for this will be the best method of imprinting such particulars in your memory." Ben was a pretty smart guy!

While in graduate school earning an MBA at Indiana University, I also served as a coach on Jerry Yeagley's soccer staff. Technically, my title was equipment manager, but I don't recall ever managing any equipment. Coach Yeagley and the Hoosier soccer program are arguably the most successful coach and college soccer program combination of all time. I learned a lot from Coach Yeagley and he treated me like part of his family. Actually, that may be the most important thing I learned from him. Treat people like family and you will receive their absolute loyalty.

Each fall as I prepared for midterms and final exams, I created flash cards to help me study. During several games, I had the flashcards in my pocket as I sat on the bench. Every time the ball went out of bounds, I would flip through a few flash cards to drive concepts deeper into my mind so it would be nearly impossible for me to produce wrong answers on tests. The process worked! I finished my MBA experience as a top student.

A few years ago I watched an interview with a University of Connecticut Huskies women's basketball player. She was asked about her coach, the one and only, coach Geno Auriemma. Coach Auriemma has led UConn to eleven NCAA Division I national championships, the most in women's collegiate basketball history, and he has won eight national Naismith College Coach of the Year awards. He has an incredible track record of success. When this player was asked what makes coach Auriemma's approach different than others, she replied "Coach doesn't make us do things until we get them right. He makes us do them until we can't get them wrong."

I have given you two examples of the incredible power of "over-learning."

However, reading ideas is one thing, putting ideas into practice is the key. You need to over-learn them. A coach early in my soccer playing "career" told me, "A skill is not a skill until you use it in a game." Or, as Frank Sinatra said when he forgot to sing his part at the appropriate time, "Stop, stop. I was reading the notes. You can't just read the notes. You've got to sing them." There are lots of ways to be an over-learner. Find what works for you and do it.

Here are some concepts from this book that you might want to consider over-learning:

**Do you have good answers to the following questions?**
- o   Who?
- o   How?
- o   Why?

**Is your organization A.R.M.ed for battle?**

**Are you employing P.RA.I.S.E. in your daily work as a leader?**

**Have you paid attention to all four quadrants of four-D Leadership this past week?**

**Have you deployed "See Something, Say Something" by praising the work of each of your teammates in the past seven days?**

**Are you and your team battling adversity or success?** You will always face one or the other. Whichever it is, are you calling the plays required to address your current reality?

**Are you helping your teammates find solutions by asking questions?** Remember, the question is the answer.

**Are you leading by remote control?**

**Are you leading with S.O.F.T. to let the game be the teacher?**

**Are you encouraging a culture of T.R.U.S.T. and collaboration?**

**Are you using commitment as your tool for motivating your team?**

**Are you and your team maintaining a growth (versus acceptance) mindset to reap the rewards of the Get-Better Mentality?**

**Are you investing in R&D to get even better?**

**Are you leveraging the P.O.W.E.R. of emotional intelligence to get win-win results through others?**

## Play to win!

On December 6, 1987, I was on a bus headed to play San Diego State in the collegiate national championship. I was seated next to our team captain, Paul Rutenis, who to this day remains one of my dearest friends. Our Clemson Tiger soccer team was the last team selected for the 1987 NCAA tournament and we had overcome nearly impossible odds to reach the final. We had beaten Evansville, perennial power Indiana, and Rutgers, featuring American soccer icon Alexi Lalas, all on the road. We had also come off a 4 – 1 thumping of North Carolina in the semi-finals. North Carolina had previously dismantled us in similar fashion during the regular season in Chapel Hill.

We were ready to work our tails off for ninety minutes and if we didn't win, we would be left with nothing. As we made the trek from the hotel to historic Riggs Field in Clemson, South Carolina, Paul turned to me and said, "We have to play the game anyway, we might as well win it." At that moment, the philosophy for my life was completely crystallized. I made a commitment right then and there: "In everything I do, I'm going to always play to win."

Life is hard. To compete requires a tremendous amount of effort. However, it takes just a bit more to be victorious. There is very little traffic on the extra mile. Be an optimist, over-learn, create raving fans, and faithfully apply the other tools in this book to achieve outstanding results. Make a commitment to play to win in everything. To do this, simply say the following words out loud and repeat them daily: "In everything I do, I'm going to always play to win." I said that thirty years ago and it has made all the difference for me.

Now it's your turn to practice the approaches you feel are most valuable and relevant for you and your situation; those that will help you achieve consistent business success. This book is a gift to the world. I am honored that you have taken the time to read it. My greatest hope is that the ideas here generate similar, or even more success for you in your career and in your life.

I wish you and your family all the best.


Your friend,


Jamey Rootes

# Acknowledgments

There are so many people to thank who contributed to the creation of this book. To my beautiful wife Melissa, thank you for always believing in me and for encouraging me throughout this process. I can't imagine walking this journey through life without you.

To my son Chris, thank you for changing my life. When you were born my capacity to love went to a new level and I am so proud to be your dad.

To my daughter Caroline, thank you for introducing me to the magic of a daughter's love. I will always be your biggest fan.

To my parents Jack and Maurine, thank you for helping me discover my talents and for convincing me that I can do and be anything. I love you.

To my brother John, thank you for always being a great role model for me. I credit our sibling rivalry for the creation of my competitive fire which still burns brightly today.

To Bob, Janice, Cal, Hannah, and the McNair family, thank you for being amazing champions for Houston and for giving all of us Texans the resources and support required to be great.

To Lamar, Norma, Clark, Tavia, Dan, and the Hunt family, thank you for giving me an opportunity to pursue my dreams. I am so happy that you earned a World Championship with the Kansas City Chiefs earlier this year. You deserve the very best because you are the gold standard for being amazing stewards of what you view as "community assets."

To my Texans teammates over the past two decades, thank you for being the key element in our Houston Texans machine that is laser focused on winning championships, creating memorable experiences, and doing great things for Houston. You are my extended family and I am so proud to be your teammate.

Thank you to Scott McClelland, my dear friend and one of the most effective leaders I have ever known. I've learned a lot from you and appreciate you more than you know.

I also want to thank my friends who took the time to provide critical feedback during the writing process, including Naren Aryal, Ashley Browder, Bob Charlet, Lee DeLeon, Bob Harvey, John Johnson, Bill McKeon, Peter Remington, John Rootes (my favorite brother), Lisa Shumate, and Michelle Wildgen (my sweet sister-in-law). Thank you for your time and your brutal honesty. You definitely made this book much better.

And I extend a special thank you to Ashley Browder, Allie LeClair, and Bonny Marshall who went above and beyond to make sure that this project stayed on schedule and I did not embarrass myself too much. You ladies are very special to me.

Lastly, I have to thank my amazing publishing team of Melanie Johnson, Anita Henderson, and Jenn Foster who worked diligently with me to make this book a reality. Thank you for your hard work, insight, and encouragement.

To those who I have not specifically mentioned, but deserve recognition, I apologize for the oversight and I thank you for your support. Herc's to you!

# About the Author

Jamey Rootes has served as president of the Houston Texans since the team's inception in 1999. Under his leadership the Texans have consistently been recognized as one of the most valuable professional sports franchises in the NFL and globally, as designated by a variety of business publications. Under Rootes' leadership, the Texans extended their sold-out game streak to one hundred, eighty-five consecutive home games, a Houston NFL record and a testament to his development of the team's highly acclaimed customer service strategy and fan gameday experience.

Rootes has taken a hands-on approach to all business functions of the club, including securing stadium naming rights and sponsorship, coordinating radio and TV broadcasting relationships, engineering the club's successful ticket and suite sales campaigns, and leading the creation and launch of the team's identity. During Rootes' tenure, the Texans have earned many distinctions, including numerous "Crystal Awards" presented by the American Marketing Association, and two American Business Awards for marketing excellence. J.D. Power recognized the team for providing the best fan experience in the NFL, and featured the Texans as a service success story in their book entitled *Satisfaction: How Every Great Company Listens to the Voice of the Customer*. The Texans have also been recognized with *Sports Business Journal*'s PRISM Award, which is given annually to the top major professional sports team based on business excellence criteria.

He also serves as president of Lone Star Sports & Entertainment (LSSE), a sports management agency associated with the Texans. LSSE has been a catalyst for some of Houston's most significant sporting events, including collegiate events such as the Texas Bowl and the Texas Kickoff annual college football game, as well as soccer games such as COPA America in 2016, the Manchester Derby in 2017, and an International Champions Cup match between Real Madrid and Bayern Munich in 2019.

Jamey Rootes has been one of Houston's leading executives for more than two decades. *Sports Business Journal* twice selected him as a member of its distinguished "Forty Under 40" list of leading sports executives, and in 2014 he was named a finalist for Executive of the Year by The Stadium Business Awards. In 2019, Rootes was selected as one of *Houston Business Journal*'s Most Admired CEOs and was selected in 2016 as the first-ever *Houston Business Journal*'s Business Person of the Year after serving as chairman of the Greater Houston Partnership. Rootes served on the Super Bowl Host Committees in 2004 and 2017 and was appointed deputy chairman of two public boards for Super Bowl LI. Rootes led the efforts to secure the Texans' appearance on Monday Night Football in Mexico for the first time in NFL history and elevated Houston's visibility on an international scale.

He maintains an active role in the community by serving on the Board of Directors of the Greater Houston Partnership and the United Way of Greater Houston. He also oversees the activities of the Houston Texans Foundation, whose mission is to be "Champions for Youth." Rootes has consistently been at the forefront of disaster recovery, including in response to COVID-19 and Hurricane Harvey, working with local organizations to raise millions in relief for Houstonians.

Prior to joining the Texans, Rootes helped launch Major League Soccer as president and general manager of the Columbus Crew. During his tenure, the Crew was consistently among the league's strongest teams both on and off the field. Rootes was recognized as MLS's Executive of the Year in 1996 and Marketing Executive of the Year in 1999. He helped lead the construction of Crew Stadium in 1999, which was the first stadium of its type in the United States. This facility earned distinction as America's Foremost Sports Facility of the Year and led to the development of numerous soccer-specific stadiums across the United States, including BBVA Compass Stadium in Houston.

A native of Stone Mountain, Georgia, Rootes graduated *cum laude* from Clemson University's Calhoun Honors College. While attending Clemson, Rootes was a member of the Tigers soccer team that captured two NCAA titles, and he served as Student Body President. While earning a Master's of Business Administration (MBA) with honors at Indiana University, he served as an assistant soccer coach for the Hoosiers. Rootes previously held positions at IBM and Procter & Gamble before entering sports. He lives in West University with his wife Melissa, and their children, Chris and Caroline.

CPSIA information can be obtained
at www.ICGtesting.com
Printed in the USA
LVHW050027290121
677617LV00005B/277